Sidewalks in the Jungle

What it's REALLY Like to Retire and Live in Costa Rica

Sidewalks in the Jungle

What it's REALLY Like to Retire and Live in Costa Rica

Alfred Stites

Hatala Geroproducts • Greentop, Missouri

Sidewalks in the Jungle: What it's REALLY Like to Retire and Live in Costa Rica
by Alfred Stites

ISBN-13: 978-1-933167-33-6

LCCN: 2008927133

Interior Photos: Alfred Stites
Cover Design: Bryan De Guzman
Cover Photo: Mark Hatala
Composition: Age Positive Design

To my dearly loved Toni

Table of Contents

Supplement

Preface

Things in Costa Rica are simply not as they are presented in the travel books, and expatriates do have a lot of problems trying to establish a life here. After the third couple we knew decided to move to another Central or South American country simply because of the difficulties here, I decided to write about what is really happening in this lovely country. This book is my own opinion and observation; I write what I see and know.

Be sure that with all the complications, we do enjoy the life here. Of course, we are not investing in real estate – the major investment we made was in a 16 year old car – we don't have a business, we just enjoy a simple life and can laugh at the rest. We have learned to accept the difficulties as part of living, as the Ticos do. We enjoy the *pura vida* side, the *tranquilo* life, knowing that this country is really struggling with the extraordinary growth problems that come with a developing country that is developing too fast. If there are those in Costa Rica that take umbrage at some of the revelations here, I trust that such revelations might just spur the government and the people to do something about the problems. They are all solvable, and with the will of the public to work for a better CR, they will be overcome.

A sidewalk in the jungle

Introduction

When my wife Toni and I moved to this beautiful country called "The Paradise of Central America," all the information we had on what it would be like to live here were two or three travel-to-Costa Rica books we had skimmed through at a bookstore. However, once the word got out we were moving, perfect strangers would contact us about how lovely it was, and really how cheap it is to live there, and how wonderful the beaches are. Everything was said to be perfect. That was the word on Costa Rica!

Arriving here with four suitcases of clothes and twenty-four boxes of books and mementos to follow, we realized from day one we really did not know anything about what it was like here. The travel books mentioned all the fine restaurants and exotic tourist sites, but the books glossed over any difficulties and smoothed past the real problems.

In this book about living in "Paradise" the ragged edges are revealed – the big problems and some of the many, many little ones. I acknowledge them with a humorous twist, and a little sardonic bent here and there as I recount the inability of this bureaucracy to make even the simplest things happen. In between the chapters I intersperse stories of our actual experiences. Some of them are hilarious, some are a little pathetic, and some you won't believe.

At first blush, when we were being welcomed into this different society, Ticos seemed to be a natural, warm and gracious people with little artifice, and this Costa Rica seemed to be a lovely and interesting place. We came to realize that a person has to be wealthy enough to live independently in order to be above the problems in the rest of the country. Or, a person must become as near Tico (the native Costa Rican) as possible in his approach to life in order to survive with some grace. Having acclimatized with the latter approach, we do enjoy being here, albeit the sometimes outrageous and always frustrating happenings that are recounted. And yes, there is a real sidewalk in the jungle near our home on the slopes of a volcano. It typifies some aspects of this government – it goes nowhere, and seemingly has no purpose.

To give you some perspective when reading about this country, here are the details:

- CR is a shade over 51,000 sq. miles. – about the size of West Virginia

- It has a little more than 4 million population – close to half of the people live in and around the capital San Jose in the Central Valley. They call themselves "Ticos".

- There are seven Provinces and dozens of cantones (counties).

- The other major cities are Alajuela - ¾ mill., Cartago – ½ mill., Puntarenas – 370 thous., and Heredia 125 thous. (all approximate).

- The currency is the Colon. In the summer of 2008 – 515 to the dollar.

- There are two seasons to this tropical and subtropical climate: Wet (May -Nov.) and Dry (Dec.– April)

• It is hot at the beaches and cool in the mountains.

• Oscar Arias is the president of this Social Democracy;
     there is no army; all children must attend primary
     school, all must become literate, all can
     vote at age 18. It is termed a "developing" nation.

• The economy is 50% tourism, the rest based on
     agriculture and electronics (Intel) export. The
     average wage for personal services is 750 colons/hr.
     – about $1.50. Imports are taxed very highly
     (to induce you to buy locally).

• It has been recognized as one of the most rapidly
     growing economies in the world, with the
     north Pacific Coast called the "gold coast" of
     Costa Rica.

• Statistics have accounted for 182 slums in the San Jose
     metropolitan area, and 208 in the rest of the
     country. And the slums here are really pitiful.

• It is recognized as one of the most beautiful countries
     in the world with exceptional ecosystems.

Coffee pickers

The Casual People

Every country is a different slice of humanity, and there is a different "take" on how one survives in that society. When that culture is "developing" (as economists term Costa Rica), the results are both charming and frustrating.

In the first week of feeling out this new environment I said "Costa Rica (CR as we most often call it) is like the U.S. used to be fifty years ago." It is, in the way people are friendly, the few regulations on everyday activities, the easiness and carefree, casual attitude that pervades this land. Being a senior (as are most expatriates here) I remember those days of taking food to new neighbors, always stopping to help a stranger with a problem and similar acts of good neighbors. It was a people-oriented life.

Twenty-first century life in Costa Rica, however, has its cautions, like most societies in the world these days – such as the necessity to lock one's doors at night, always having the front gate locked against strangers, and more. There is the "affluent" and "poor" division here just like anywhere, although one of the differences in CR is that the one-room tin shelter of the poor may be right next to the fine mansion of the affluent, thus economic divisions are more obvious.

CR has very few regulations. You will get the feeling that you are really free in this little country. There are no signs telling you what you cannot do. In a restaurant you don't smoke if there are no ashtrays on the tables (only 15% of the population smokes). There are no "don't" signs around: don't – walk on the grass, cross here, enter here, touch this, open this, etc. etc. as in the U.S. Ticos habitually don't do something that may be abusive or intrusive to the environment or to other people.

The gentle side of these Ticos (their own nickname – no slur) harkens back to the 1950's as well – being polite. On our first bus ride two teenagers got up to give us their seat! They still do that for old people and women! When the school buses are loading up the boys wait until all the girls are onboard. And should you drop something while you are walking downtown people stop, pick it up, and run after you to give it back. When your car is stuck in the road other cars stop and come over to see if they can help. There is an instinctive politeness and graciousness. One of the many customs is that men shake hands each time they meet. They may have had breakfast together, or be lifelong friends, but when they see each other again during the day they shake hands hello. A shop owner will walk through the shop and shake hands with each employee each morning when he comes in. When you get to see the clerk in the local *ferreteria* (hardware) store more than a few times you always shake hands with him when you go in. And you always ask how he is – the *Como esta?*

For the ladies there is kissing on the cheek. When you are introduced to a total stranger you kiss her on the right cheek. And when you part, again the kiss. A very pleasant custom.

If you ask for directions to find a place you want to visit, you will get answers! In no time several people will be telling you how to get where you are going. Most of them will be wrong, to be sure, but everyone wants to help. It would be rude for a man to say to you "I don't know" when you have asked for directions, so you get an answer : "It is that way … maybe six kilometers, that way." And, of course, you drive ten kilometers and find nothing;

you ask someone else and they point you in the opposite direction. It is lovely talking to all these nice people, and very frustrating. When I say "talk" you had better have some Spanish because very few people speak English outside the major metropolitan hotels and resorts, regardless of what the travel books say.

Their treatment of the elderly also harkens back to an earlier America. Anyone over seventy is accorded special treatment. In any bank or government office the old guy goes immediately to the head of the line. Except, as a matter of fact, at MOPD where you get your driver's license! There you could be using a walker and they would wait until you finally got to the No.1 position, then they'd ring down the curtain and tell you to come back tomorrow and do it all over again. But then that bureau is the same in every country, isn't it?

Another pleasant aspect of the people here is their dress. When Ticos are out and about shopping or going to visit friends, etc. they are neatly dressed and clean. To be sure, most of the women (seeming from age fourteen on) have ample bosoms, and the young women are voluptuous and generous in displaying their physical attributes. The girls wear the tightest and shortest skirts and the skimpiest blouses seen on the planet (having traveled thorough 22 countries I am an authority on this). How the so-called "hip-huggers" stay on is beyond physics. Not having the Puritan strictures that have afflicted the U.S. for two centuries, the breasts are not something that must be hidden and denied. These women show all the flesh and cleavage they can demonstrate.

One rarely sees hats or sunglasses and everyone carries an umbrella in the rainy season. The young men, the teenagers, do **not** wear those baggy pants that drag in the dirt nor do they wear the torn, ripped, or worn jeans that seem to be the fashion in the

U.S. Most people wear "quiet" clothes, no loud colors and stripes; the men wear their T-shirts inside their trousers, the older women wear more skirts than slacks, and the clothes are generally of a dark shade – lighter colors mean more dirt, which means more washing. The fact that not many wear sunglasses does not deter the "hawkers" – in every city and town in CR, wherever there is a stoplight and traffic must pause, there are those ubiquitous sellers of everything from food to sunglasses.

The Tico politeness carries over in conversation. When you greet someone – in person or on the telephone – you must always ask how they are. Their house could be burning down, but first you must ask how they are and respond to their similar question of you, and then you tell them to please return home because of the fire. The politeness and courtesy of everyone can be frustrating. For example, when you go to a store that carries small tanks of propane gas for the stove, they may be out of tanks, but they immediately say "They will be in tomorrow." The clerk has no idea whether the tanks will be back in stock the next day or not. That is the response you are always given, no matter what you are looking for. And, of course, the tanks will not be in tomorrow as you will find out when you drive down to the store the next day! You will again be told "They will be in tomorrow."

When you call up a supplier of propane for your hot water heater and ask for a delivery of a large tank the following day you are always told, "Absolutely, we will be there in the afternoon." You suggest an approximate time and the response is "Absolutely, we'll be there at that time!" Of course, it is not delivered the next day, and when you call up you get no apology or explanation but are told "Tomorrow, absolutely." Two or three days later the delivery truck will show up – when you are not at home! You will get used to this interesting way to live.

Of course, there are the long-time expatriates, who have become cynical, who say that they do not treat other Ticos that way, just *Norte Americanos*, and that they are putting us on, that they will cheat an American whenever they think they can get away with it. And from some of our experiences it may be so.

When you go to a store to get something and find they do not carry it, and you ask who does, you can be sure you will be told where to find it. And you can be equally sure that when you drive and follow the convoluted directions and finally find the place they will not have it either. And they will tell you someplace else!

This style of living is responsible for much of the casual attitude of deliveries, or getting something for you, or doing something for you. We have Tico friends who are absolutely lovely people, and they mean everything they tell you when they promise to assist you in some manner. They may promise to come over the next day but the next day they do not show up, nor do they call and say some event happened and they cannot come. There are no apologies, it is just that they wanted **at the time** to be of assistance, but on the next day something else came up. Quite natural.

On the other hand, many times their generosity and kindness will exceed your most hopeful expectations. We had a call from our landlord who had just visited after we had moved to our second house here and were told "I am sending a truck up to you with some chairs for your veranda" and the truck arrives with two absolutely lovely rockers for the patio. Free. Not to be returned. A gift.

And when we first came here we had no car and used busses for whatever travel we needed. A neighbor (U.S. expat) apparently saw us walking down our dirt road carrying the striped plastic bags that every store supplies to carry your food and called us up and said "The next time you want to go to the store, give us a call, you can use our car." They had lived here for enough years to have been inculcated with the Tico attitude toward sharing with one's neighbors. When we finally did get a used car and it immediately went into the shop for repairs (normal – see the chapter on "Traveling the Roads"), another friend dropped by with the keys to their second car – told us to use it as long as we needed to. How many times have you been offered the use of your neighbor's car when he saw you walking down the street?

When we moved into our first rented house we were told the house would never be sold, the owners would keep it as an investment and we could stay as long as we wished. We rented the 1,500 square foot house unfurnished, and we had no furniture, but our new landlord had a furniture factory and promised to make all the furniture and deliver it in a week, no charge! We lived for two weeks with two plastic chairs, a cardboard box for a table, and a pallet with a mattress to sleep on – and a deck of cards (my wife and I get along pretty well). Of course, this was our introduction to "Tico Time" since the furniture got delivered a piece at a time over the next several weeks. Our bed was first, then four chairs, then a dining room table, then a second bed, etc., etc. In a few months we were happily settled in!

My wife loves plants, and by the second month of our living here she had a dozen plants scattered around the house that she had gathered from local greenhouses. One Saturday afternoon a pickup truck pulled up in our driveway piled high and chock full of greenery. A young English-speaking woman popped out of the truck and called out "Hi, I'm Maria and I'm moving to

Panama and my sister told me someone told her that one of your neighbors said you love plants so you can have these." We still have the two ten foot high rubber plants, a larger Fica Tree, and dozens and dozens of plants of all kinds. Lovely people.

The house we were living in was sold after two years. The promise of permanence for us was sincere at the time, but things change, don't they? Although we could stay there for however many months it look for us to find another place – the laws here favor the renters – we decided not to hold up the sale for our nice landlords and luckily found an absolutely wonderful new home right away (the one where we were given the veranda rockers). I called my landlord and told him we would move out by the end of the week, and I needed to discuss the cost of the furniture with him because we did need it, since our new house was rented empty. Our landlord said "No, you don't owe us anything, and all the furniture is yours for as long as you live in Costa Rica. If you ever leave the country, then you can return it." Now that is being kind, gracious, and just plain nice!

One cannot leave the subject of the people here without a mention of the children. Honestly, we were here over a year before we heard a child crying. The kids in the school yards, on the street, playing *futbol* (soccer) in the empty field after school are always happy, laughing, and just enjoying each other. They watch out for their younger siblings and are dutiful and responsible when left with chores to do. Obviously, the family here is a strong and cohesive element. I thought that religion would play a large part, but although the country is 95% Roman Catholic, only about 25% of the people attend church regularly. It just seems that since in most of the families the wife does not work they have the time to raise the children with respect for elders, the law, good manners, courtesy and kindness for others, and the customs of the country. I have never seen a parent show anger or disrespect to his child, either. We were told by our first attorney "We Ticos work as little as possible so we can enjoy life and our families as much as possible." Quite a difference from the U.S. standard of working as much as possible to make as much money as possible so they can enjoy life when they retire – the children too many times having to raise themselves.

The quiet and firm discipline is present in public as well as family life. All school children wear uniforms, and there are two sets of classes per day. Children can run wild and screaming with laughter on the playground, but they are behaved and courteous when out shopping with their parents. Unfortunately, one of the politicians here, who must have studied U.S. "political correctness," has recently introduced a bill to punish parents for spanking their children! It will fail with a resounding crash.

Costa Rica has few problems as yet with teenage drinking and drugs. Most probably it is because the children are raised by full-time parents, and the fact that there is very little divorce in this Catholic country. There is about 7% unemployment, and youngsters must pass a literacy test in reading and writing. The government prides itself is saying there is 99% literacy here. There are government schools, private kindergartens, day schools, high schools, and many colleges and universities of all types throughout the land. The government gives 5% of its gross income over to education, and they subsidize schools of all kinds. All children must go to school until they are 16. However, many of the San Jose and other major city kids – the lower income kids – drop out at 16 even though they have not gone through to grade 12. In this school system if they do not meet the standards they do not get promoted! A novel idea, and the way the U.S. once was (now it's "don't hurt the child's delicate psyche just because he is 14, smokes dope, and won't learn to read!").

The other side of the education coin is that the government does not have enough money to provide even the essentials for educating a child. Too many schools have no school books, not to mention pencils and paper for the children. Some public schools rely on the community volunteers to give money to buy these essentials. When a school gets computers donated by some international company it is headlined in the paper with no questions as to why the CR government cannot provide for its people. In the really rural areas the lack of facilities and simple basic teaching tools are pretty standard. The government's heralded 5% GNP for education is just not enough to provide a building for all the schools and all the children. Of course, as in almost every country in the world, the teachers are not paid enough and periodically go on a protest strike for a day or so. It should also be mentioned that this system attempts to provide education, not job training – the children are all taught a second language, a choice between English and French with their math, history, geography and science. When they get out of school the English will be a great help in getting a job, the French will not. But, if there is no typing competence, no computer knowledge or other essentials for this modern world, the child cannot get a job, and so takes whatever menial situation is available. Those who go on to university fare a great deal better in that they perfect their English and focus on an occupation area.

All is not peaches and cream in family life, either. It seems that in this country, as in any of the countries with low income where the poverty line is **very** poor and where a large family may live in a small house, there is abuse of daughters by fathers, siblings, even lovers of the mother, (one expat told me that as many of the women here have lovers as do the men). The country has an excellent department of social services – the P.A.N.I. – that quickly removes a child from an abusive situation – if they hear about it.

That agency has hundreds of homes throughout the country, and an average of 12 children per home ages one month to 18 years. The kids receive clean clothes, basic food, and the barest elements needed for school. When they are 18 they must leave the home. Growing up inside a controlled environment they have been taught little understanding of the "outside" world. They have little social contact; they go shopping, sometimes only a few times a year. When they are released from the system neither the boys nor girls have had job training, or know anything about how to get a job! Unless an individual gets lucky and someone knows someone of the family and can get a job for the boy he will turn to thievery. And with no alternative the 18 year old girl will likely become a prostitute. Someday someone will get a grant and talk the local corporations and businesses into setting up a job training program and save hundreds of lives a year.

Also, there is legal prostitution in CR. Since we don't go into San Jose at night, nor do we frequent the casinos (legal gambling too), we see few ladies "standing on the corner watching all the boys go by." There was a big concern for a while about the number of U.S. men coming to CR for underage sex. It died down for a while as the publicity shined the light on the traffickers and the police did make arrests. In a recent press conference the President admitted that CR " … is considered one of the top sex tourism destinations of the world." And CR has recently gotten some international notice for being a country where there is too much of this. As for drugs, well, as in almost every country, marijuana is illegal, but is everywhere. CR has become a transfer point and refueling stop. The hard drugs skip in and out of Costa Rica, mainly on the way to Mexico and the easy passage into the U.S. with little border control. Drug volume is way up in this country, and it has become visible in the beach communities and San Jose, while still somewhat in the shadows in the other smaller cities and towns.

San Jose city street

Car Repair
Chaos Triumphant

In this land of pleasant people who seem to be unable to give you a less than positive answer to anything, it becomes a challenge (requiring the Divinity of God's Wisdom and the hard reality of a professional gambler) to have one's automobile repaired in Costa Rica.

When our new friends John and Sally saw us without transportation and facing the tedium of riding the buses whenever we wanted to shop or visit, they insisted we use their second car whenever we wanted. We happily accepted, knowing that we would take good care of their largess. When a slight shimmy developed in the steering – inevitable due to the ubiquitous potholes that have made wheel alignment shop owners upper class citizens – we would drive into a garage we had noticed in passing and have the problem adjusted. That we always were admonished to replace one or two tires or shocks, or ball joints along with the alignment, was a given. Something always needs replacement when driving into a garage here. It is a credo passed from father to son in this trade.

However, after a year or so living in this embracing Costa Rica where the people are gentle, seemingly so friendly and honest, one becomes inclined to accept whatever is pronounced, by even a mechanic, as gospel, even though in the back of the mind a voice says *He is a mechanic who always wants to do more work, so ask more questions!* And, if the garage owner speaks fairly good English, one is even more inclined to accept whatever judgments are pronounced about the condition of the automobile. He's "half American!"

It was when we took the plunge and purchased our own used car that our experiences began to expand. We bought a 1986 Jeep Cherokee from an American expatriate who was returning to the U.S. after ten years. The car was in excellent condition inside and out which lent credence to our thinking *If such good care has been taken of the body, surely the engine must have received equal care.* By the way, one never buys a nearly new used car here because of the road conditions. An automobile always needs repair after a few months of driving, and more complicated newer models just require more complicated repairs.

We also had the confidence that a fellow American would not knowingly mislead us in so important a purchase. The fact that he had operated a Sports Book in one of the local casinos did not register with any significance – here, working Americans all seem to have unusual occupations. So after a test drive around the block, the car seemed to be "just fine." It did stall a couple of times – "The motor is a little cold" he said, and there was some difficulty getting the 4-wheel drive to work "I haven't used it for months so it probably is a little stiff" he said. We bought the car. Our confidence increased when the owner lowered the price $500 if we would allow him to drive it for his final two weeks in country. If he wanted to use it for a few more weeks, well then, we knew the car was in good working order.

Two weeks later to the day we picked up our "new" car, handed over the purchase price, and for the next weeks we drove our car happily to the stores, to visit friends, and even to the shore for our first holiday. Except for some stalling, which seemed to grow in frequency as the days passed, and for a seeming lack of power when we drove up and around the hills, the car was enjoyed and these little annoyances were overlooked. It did seem to use a lot of gas, however, and with fuel being $2.80 a gallon this could become a concern. But when it began stalling a half a dozen times in a mile when driving around corners, when turning, when coming to a stop, we decided to take it to the local mechanic Jorge Campo, who had been referred to us by a couple of local U.S. expatriates, and friends of ours as "a good mechanic, an honest man."

Jorge Campo spoke no English, but since my wife has learned quite a bit of the language now, we got our message about the car's problem across to the smiling man. He asked us to leave it and to come back in a day or two after he could evaluate the problem. I should explain that having lived here for six months we knew that "a day or two" could mean a week. Time has no meaning in this country. I am sure that Jorge confidently expected to check out our car in a day or two, but should something else come up, or if he decided to take a week off, then the car would have to wait. It is just the way things are.

Sometime that week, however, we did get a call to come down to his shop, about a mile down the mountain. It was with a sad face that Jorge Campo told us that the problem was the engine was getting no compression, and that we needed to have the **engine rebuilt**!

This required time to seep into my consciousness: *We needed a Rebuilt Engine! A Jeep engine, with 186,000 miles, had simply worn out? Too bad. Nothing else to do. Rebuilt engine. The cost would be $500. Wow, if we were in the States this would cost $2000!* "Well, Okay, Jorge, if that's what you think has to be done *(everyone says this guy is honest)*, well then, go ahead and do it. How long will it take?"

J.C. (since we had placed our transportation fates in his hands he had acquired more than human status) looked at the ground for a moment or two, shook his head, sighed, and said "Oh, two or three weeks, at least. It depends."

I knew by this time it would "depend" on how much new Tico work came in when he was working on our car. But my wife and I looked at each other saying with our eyes, "What other choice do we have?" Obviously, our other choice would have been to go to another mechanic and see what he thought. *But would another CR mechanic be any more responsible than good 'ole J.C.? Probably not. Everyone says he is honest.*

"Okay, Jorge Campo," we said as I handed over the requested $250 half for this major job. (He needed the advance to pay the shops in San Jose who would actually do the re-boring and valve grinding – a not unusual request here). "I will call you" he said and smiled as we left.

It was during this period that our friends John and Sally (described above) insisted we use their second car. Two months and one week later (after many repeated stops at the garage to inquire about the progress) good 'ole J.C. drove up our drive with our rebuilt Jeep! We noticed that it did stall as he turned in the drive, but he said it was "just cold" as we gave over the remaining $250. We had our car back! We had a practically new car!

That afternoon we called up John and Sally and told them we would be over for a drink – we had our car. As we drove that 1 km trip through our village the car stalled each time I made a left turn. Also, it did not seem to have much power going up a hill. We took the car back to J.C. the next day and explained the problem to him. He nodded thoughtfully, and said to leave it for a few days and he would check it out.

Two days later we got a call, went down to the garage and saw our jeep sitting in the rear of the shop, hood up, and a part sitting on the floor. The carburetor. Jorge said the car needed a **rebuilt carburetor**, that this one was worn out, no good. It would cost around 55,000 colones ($135.00) because he could not get a Jeep carburetor in Costa Rica, but would adapt one from a Toyota. It would take a few weeks.

We got the car back in three weeks. We paid for the "new" rebuilt Toyota carburetor as J.C. held up our old one saying in English: "No good, no good." We drove away and the car stalled three times on the short drive home. That night we were having drinks with John and Sal, who then suggested we call "Carl," a U.S. mechanic who has lived here for ten years, and who "stands behind his work." He had had a shop in New York State and decided to come here to live so he could play golf and work sometimes. But, "He is really a good mechanic." *Why was this man not recommended to us before? Well, probably because living here means everyone is responsible for his own actions, and other people simply do not interfere unless asked.*

"Okay, we'll try him." I called Carl the next day. He quickly informed me he plays golf Tuesday, Thursday and Saturday in the mornings and to bring the car in Monday after 1:00 pm. We did.

Carl is a very personable guy. He casually addressed what we must have gone through – trying to find a Tico (CR) mechanic who knew what he was doing and was honest as well – thus establishing himself as one who was both. We left the car with him. The next day the phone rang and Carl said "Can you get your old carburetor back? And the air filter?" I said I thought I could still get it, but J.C. had said it was no good. Carl casually said "Well, maybe I can rebuild it because the Toyota carburetor he gave you is too small for this car, it won't work well on a Jeep. Oh, by the way, did you say the engine was rebuilt?" I replied, "Yes, it took the local guy two months." He said, "Hmm. It sure doesn't look as if the bolts were ever removed from the head. They have 5 years dirt on them. Well, it could be that your man just doesn't wipe his bolts. Or something." *Well, by damn, the sumbitch J.C. wiffled me!*

I went back to a smiling J.C. and said nothing – what was the point – and he looked surprised when asked for the carburetor, but retrieved it and the filter from his back shelf. We took it to Carl and 4 days later we got a call that the Jeep carburetor was rebuilt and the car was ready. Another drive in John's car back to Carl, and we were assured the car was running fine, and we should take the Toyota carburetor to J.C. and get our money back (Hah!). We paid the bill of $210 and drove away happy, back again in our car that we had driven for three weeks in the past three months.

To celebrate we accepted an offer from other friends (everyone here is so very generous) to use their condo at the shore for a week while they were away. We partnered on this small vacation with John and Sal, and this time it was *their* car in the shop – so we would drive them! It so happened that on the way to pick up supplies – requiring a drive up a steep hill – the car could barely grind its way to the top. Toni, John and Sal got out to lighten the load, and John pushed. And, the left-turn-stall was back.

John looked at me seriously and said he would borrow a car from another friend, having received an offer of a relatively new and large SUV – the word was around that the four of us were going to the shore. He quickly got on his cell phone and arranged to pick up the offered car.

We had a lovely five days at the beach, determined not to think about automobiles. When we got back, relaxed and happy, we took the car back to Carl and left it. He said he would call us.

That afternoon he said he had driven it, and the problem was the **transmission**! *Now the TRANSMISSION?* He had checked with a very reliable and large transmission shop in Santa Domingo that guaranteed the work (not a little local guy to be sure!), and it was agreed that this was a transmission problem.

We took the car in to the transmission shop owner Miguel, an expatriate from Cuba via Florida who had had a transmission business in the States and who was touted as "the best in Costa Rica." He also was a very personable man who owned this large garage (fourteen cars were in various stages of repair). Miguel said he would have the car repaired in a week. One week later we got a call – the car was ready. We paid another $555 and I drove the car home. It stalled when turning to the left. We took the car back the next day to Miguel with our six-month guarantee in hand. He test drove it, got out of the car and said, "This is not a transmission problem. It is the **carburetor** ... something is wrong with getting gas to the engine when the car turns left." *(How could a steering problem be the carburetor?).* I tried to question him several times about the work on the transmission, but Miguel kept saying "Don't worry about the transmission, it's the carburetor." *All right. It's the frigging carburetor! Well, back to our friend Carl.* By this time I am really getting steamed!

After calling to be assured Carl was not on the golf course, we drove over and he greeted us with "It could be that the timing was screwed up when they worked on the transmission." *(Does the timing have anything to do with the transmission?)* He worked on the timing for twenty minutes, adjusting and more adjusting. Finally, he got in the car with us and test-drove it up hills, around left turns, slamming to a jolting stop, and otherwise really wringing the car out. It worked fine. Except that when he parked it on the slope of his drive with the auto shift in "park" the car started drifting backward! He quickly got on the phone with Transmission Miguel and explained the situation. Miguel said "No problem. Tell them to bring it right over, it's a ten minute repair."

We drove right over and again greeted the smiling Miguel who told us to wait. It was 2:30 in the afternoon as he drove the car in the shop and we saw a young mechanic start jacking up the car. Toni and I sat on the curb and played "pitch stone" at a piece of paper in the street. (I lost a theoretical $4.75). At 4:30 pm we asked Miguel if there was time for us to get a cup of coffee and he smilingly assured us there was still just a little more to be done, so we walked to a small café and enjoyed two cups of coffee while we watched Spiderman in Spanish on their TV.

When we walked back to the garage Miguel came out and asked us if we could leave the car overnight as "there is still a little more that needs to be done." I looked in the garage and saw the transmission on the floor. We smiled and said "Sure, no problem. We'll call you tomorrow morning." We caught a cab for the half-hour ride home.

The next morning at 11:00 am we called and were told "The car is ready." We drove over (John again lending us his car), and were greeted by a smiling Miguel who this time handed me a Cuban cigar and said, "The car is fine" as he handed over the keys. *He must have test driven it because he has the keys in his hand, so maybe it works.*

I drove our "new" jeep home. The car did not stall once. It went smartly up the hills. When I accelerated, the car responded. You have no idea what a thrilling experience this was. The car ran smoothly and I actually got a response of power when I pressed on the accelerator! Damn! I think that this time Miguel actually repaired the transmission. *Maybe it is fixed. Maybe it is okay. Maybe we can drive it now!*

It seems we now have an automobile! We can get into our own car and drive it somewhere, to the store, to the post office, to friends, and it runs fine. To you this may seem a simple thing. To my lady and me it means we have triumphed over a worn out purchase, inept mechanics, unknowledgeable garages, and "dealing with repairs of U.S. cars in Costa Rica."

The Jeep is for sale. (We also have a used Toyota carburetor for sale since dear ole smiling J.C. said he didn't want it). The 10 miles per gallon, and the fact that it has started stalling again has worn us to the point of admitting this Jeep is not the car for us. We will sell it and get an old Datsun, or Kia, or Hyundai, that they know something about here. Maybe we will get lucky.

Burning sugar cane

Maids, Gardeners, & Caretakers

Most expats here are like us – they have a part-time gardener and housekeeper – the maid a day a week and the gardener on Sunday. You can judge the affluence of the expats in this country by the number of servants they have. We have a few good friends who have four or five full time live-on-the-premises servants (very wealthy), and we have good friends who have a fulltime maid and gardener (moderately wealthy), and we have many good friends who have a part-time maid and gardener – three or four days a week (they have a comfortable monthly income). Then there are those like us (we only know a few) who have a maid and gardener a day or two a week. The average wage here is 750 colones (about $1.50) per hour so almost everyone can afford caretakers. Maids get paid more than gardeners because good ones are **very** hard to find! And when you find a good one you make sure you treat her right and you overlook the "Tico Way," which is frustrating for all North American women at first. Ticos clean house the way their mothers taught them, and nothing on God's Green Earth will ever change them.

A small example of this intransigency is the use of modern equipment. Our very nice 40 year old, short and stocky, methodical-but-thorough maid Flora regularly swept the floors in the house, then mopped them with a wet mop, then mopped them again with some type of disinfectant that left a shine! We had all wood floors in our first house, and Toni likes the floors **clean** so we bought a modern, all metal, shiny vacuum cleaner because it was powerful enough to pick up the dirt in the seams of the wood flooring. Toni showed Flora how to use it and how great it was. She watched the demo, nodded, and went about her chores. Later on in the day came time for the floors, and Flora got out the broom and started sweeping in her usual way. She swept all the gathered dirt into a pile in each room, then got the vacuum out of the closet, plugged it in, and vacuumed up the piles of dirt. She never deterred from this method of cleaning the floors. And, of course we could not insist on a change or Flora would have quit.

There were other little differences, like her penchant for waxing the tile floors in the bathrooms and kitchen. We simply could not deter her from pouring the liquid on the mop and giving our bathroom the slipperiest floor in South America when you step out of the shower. A couple of **ZZZZZZZIIPPPPWHOA!!SPAT** on the backside, and maybe the head, and you want to throttle someone. But you don't say anything, you just buy a new floor mat with a heavier non-skid backing. We eventually had one with the tread of a Goodyear all-terrain bulldozer tire.

Another trait that seems endemic in Tico housekeepers is the breakage problem. Other expat friends have confirmed this for us. A Tico housekeeper will break things, hide the pieces, and say nothing about the damage. And, it seems that because of their strong, aggressive approach to making a house whole again, they tend to break more things than most. When our new maid Cristina cleans a room, all the furniture in the room goes out into the hall, and when she starts hauling tables with fragile ceramic horses and similar bric-a-brac on them, our determined Cristina tries to be careful but there is the inevitable bang and crash. We quickly learned to take the fragile things and put them in a drawer first. By the way, we pay her c1200 per hour – about $2.40 – which is very high pay but she cleans for only us and we consider her very special. (Her breakage is noticeably less than our first "helper." She mainly breaks broom handles with her aggressive sweeping – so far we have four broken handles awaiting the fireplace – true).

Our first gardener was Manolo, a young Nico (Nicaraguan) man who spoke not one word of English (most people do not speak English here regardless of the fact that they took it in high school – when they left it seems they forgot it all), and we did not know if he was in the country legally. Costa Rica has the same problem of illegal immigrants with Nicaragua that the U.S. does with Mexico. The larger country to our north pays an average of $.50 per hour for work, so the Nicos come here and send money home. Manolo had worked for an expat neighbor who was running out of work for him and we filled in the gap. Manolo was a treasure. Like all the men here he could build a solid cement block house for our water heater; he could make a perfect herb garden complete with plastic cover that was stable in the high winds of the dry season; he could repair almost any kind of equipment; and he was an honest, hardworking, and steady worker. We gave Manolo a lot of work and he gradually became "our gardener."

As we were told, Nicos are very reliable, and unlike Ticos, they are instinctively honest and can be relied upon to keep your house safe if you leave for a weekend or so, for a short vacation. Manolo proved exactly such a man. After almost a year of working for us, we became his surrogate parents, I'm sure, and we found, little by little, that he relied on us when he got into trouble – be it the police or an outraged husband. I have written the "Story of Manolo" and it follows this chapter. It may seem unbelievable in parts, but it's all true.

Now we have a lovely young (40) and vibrant Tico – Cristina (mentioned above), as a two-half-days-a-week housekeeper who does the most thorough job ever accomplished by a homemaker. When she cleans a room – three or four hours required depending on the size – one is almost afraid to walk into it, the place sparkles! You can be assured the ceiling has been swept! A married woman, Cristina works because she wants some extra money of her own. When we tried to get her to use our vacuum cleaner we found the same resistance. She informed us that since she used a broom there was no need of a vacuum cleaner. Inescapable logic!

Our current gardener came with the new house. We have a 15 foot high hedge all around that needs trimming year 'round, and a lovely sloping lawn to be cut. He has turned out to be a general handyman as well as gardener. He has changed the water heater for us, put in 220 volt wiring for the new dryer we bought, fixed the broken dishwasher, repaired a broken water line, and done many other repairs we have needed. We pay him 800 colones per hour (about $1.70), a little better than the going wage.

When you come to live here you will need domestic help inside and out – unless you are the type who likes to work all day! You must remember that in this country of always high humidity there will be mold growing. All over. At the high altitudes, at the beaches, and most all over the country in the rainy season you will find mold on a pair of shoes you haven't worn for two weeks; there will be mold on the ceilings, in the closets, under the bed! Just regular cleaning maintenance keeps the house and home relatively free of this nuisance, however.

After moving into a place ask your neighbors about a housekeeper, and ask any other expats you run across (and they will find you very soon after your moving here) and you should shortly get a few phone numbers. A word of caution: some housekeepers purloin small things in the house after they become comfortable working there. So it is necessary to get good references from other people with whom your new house keeper has worked – preferably *Norte Americanos*. This is ABSOUTELY necessary. You will many times do your shopping or otherwise leave the house when your maid is working, and it would not be much for an untrustworthy one to let her boyfriend in and you come home to find a lot of things missing. It has happened! But then it happens in most every country around the world. Using your head is all that is necessary. And by the way, the term *Gringos* does not have the pejorative connotation here that it does in Mexico. It is just the local way of terming North Americans.

Finally, you must get acquainted with the Costa Rican "employment laws." They are strict, and always in favor of the employee. This is a social democracy, and the people come first (what a concept!). If you have full-time help you will owe them a full month's extra pay at Christmastime; after a year you must also allow a two week paid vacation along with the many, even countless, holidays; a day for this Saint, a day for that piece of history, and they add up to umpteen vacation days throughout the year – I have heard there are seventeen! They will want those days off if you have them by the week or if you pay them by the day. If they work that day you pay double time. If you work anyone over 48 hours a week they get time and a half. And should you decide to let someone go – for what ever reason after three month's employment – you will owe from two weeks employment up, plus another few weeks of "settlement" for firing the person. It is all spelled out in the law, and a reasonably intelligent attorney (somewhat of an oxymoron here) can steer you through any questions before you start hiring. If a part-time employee is let go – one who works only a few days a week – the whole thing works proportionately. Also, you will have to provide employees insurance – INS is the company – in case of an accident. As a round figure you can say an employee costs an additional 40% more than the actually weekly earnings – just to let you know what you are getting into.

Being significantly more affluent than anyone who works for you, you will be tempted to "go the extra mile" with your employees – who you want to be happy working for you. They can tend to become "family;" you will learn all about their family and their life, if you inquire. And you can be certain that should a problem come up – a child that needs a minor operation, a car that needs repair, or some similar domestic situation – you will be asked if you will help, possibly a small loan, or something similar. You will want to, and so you will.   Just be aware that it could be part of your living here.

Roils In Paradise

If one were an optimist one could say "Well, the living here has just the same intrigues, conflicts, neighborly squabbles and irritants that come with living anywhere." Here in Costa Rica, however, such consternations are magnified. Few of us work at other than a self-imposed hobby, or writing. We have no regimen, and thus are fodder for almost any aberrant situation that comes along. Such localized difficulties are intensified because the expats are, and have to be, a closely-knit community – we are foreigners in a foreign country. When there is a neighborly squabble, it affects more than just the participants. We do depend on each other for everything from borrowing an extension ladder to combining resources to get a road fixed.

Take the latest bru-ha-ha as a prime example. Sally and John, our neighbors across the road, have had the same gardener and handyman, Manolo, for two years. He's an honest, hardworking Nicaraguan man of about 40 who has been in CR for perhaps ten years, allegedly has his permits, and has survived with modest success. They liked him and six months ago bought him a small Vespa so he could get about more easily, and save the two miles walk to work each day. He was to pay for the machine by taking half his weekly salary in cash, the rest applied to the Vespa cost. He agreed to the terms since his living costs are very minimal – his tiny one-room house rent is $37 per month and he was earning about $60 a week. Good income in this rural area.

We also pay Manolo to stay in our home overnight when we would go away for a weekend at the beach (one NEVER leaves a house empty overnight in this country) – he was that dependable – and honest. When the dry season came, however, and there was not enough work to keep Manolo busy, Sally asked us if we could give him work a few days a week, which we were happy to do since our landscaped acre needed more work than we were able to keep up with. (Also, my area of expertise has little to do with gardening). So Manolo built an herb garden shelter, a planting area shelter, assisted in transplanting, edging, and myriad other small tasks around our home. Then our work slowed down, and Manolo went to Sally and more or less demanded more work so he could get by. It happens that our neighbor is a strong and positive-minded woman and Manolo caught her on a day when she was a little out-of-sorts, without sympathy for her now sometime-gardener. She railed at him in loud and hostile terms. Manolo, the Latin male and not accustomed to such a tongue-lashing, got on his little scooter and sped away.

Now, it just so happens that at this time Manolo had been having a dalliance with the wife of his landlord, and that man learned of this state of affairs about the time of Manolo's altercation with the lady Sally. One morning shortly thereafter our gardener showed up at our door, torn and disheveled, with bruised and battered face and an eye patch, asking for assistance, saying he had been beaten up, could not go back to his house, and had not eaten for two days. We gave him clothes, fed him a meal, and sent him down the road to Jake and Lorie, where he might find a few days work.

Jake is a 45 year old Austrian by birth; Lorie is a U.S. citizen. They have lived in CR for twenty years. He is a handyman who can build a garage for you, weld anything, wire your house, repair your plumbing, and otherwise fix about anything that exists. He does like his ration of beer, and Jake is sometimes one-sheet-to-the-wind when he comes to work. That he has not electrocuted himself years ago is a testament to his self-awareness. Jake keeps a libation handy during his working day to provide the needed sustenance.

So, Manolo went to Jake, who found something for him to do, and told him he could sleep on the floor that night. He worked for Jake the next day, but that evening Manolo showed again at our door asking for something to eat, saying Jake didn't give him any food, and saying he could not stay there any more because Jake (allegedly) did not pay him. (I was pleased to see him looking clean and neat in my jeans and shirt). Well, we fed him and let him stay in our guest room that night, gave him breakfast, and told him we could not house him any more and that he would have to find his own place. He assured us he had found another house and was moving in that afternoon. I should relate here that in those weeks, when he would find work with someone, Manolo almost always was out of money, "due to be paid," etc., so would we loan him a few dollars, and he would "work it off two days next week." It also always seemed that he could manage only half a day's work in any next week, and so the loans grew until he owed us $18.00 – about twelve hours of work.

Sally had long recovered from her fleeting anger at him so we suggested to Manolo that he go and talked to Mary about more work, and that she would be fine. He was adamant, however, and said he would not talk with her ever again. He continued to pick up work somewhere, apparently, because he would show up at our house asking for cigarette money saying the usual, "I have not yet been paid." We told him that from now on he would have to work for a day, then we would give him half in cash so he had some money.

The *coup de gras*, as it were, came when Manolo presented himself at the door at 9:00 o'clock at night, anguished and tearful, saying that the police had confiscated his Vespa because he was riding without a helmet; that it was at the storage yard somewhere, and could we take him to get it and give him $10.00 to pay the charge. Of course, after Toni and I discussed the situation in hushed and aggravated tones, we got in the car. Toni did the inquiries since I don't have the language skills to deal with the police, much less ask enough questions to find where the police "storage" yard might be, and after over an hour of riding about Heredia we found the yard and retrieved the Vespa. *"No mas,"* I said to him, *"No mas!"*

Later, upon learning that Sally was at the shore (everyone in this small community of Ticos knows everything that goes on), Manolo went to John and asked for severance pay for the 2 ½ years he worked! John, who never gets upset at anything, calmly reminded Manolo that he quit, and thus was owed nothing, and that Manolo still owed $800 on the Vespa. Two nights after that final confrontation, the Wilson's shed was broken into, the chain saw, the weed whacker, and other small tools were stolen. Since this kind of petty theft happens all the time to almost everyone, there is really nothing the police can, or will, do. One accepts this as part of living here in Costa Rica. While his name was not mentioned, the knowing glances that accompanied "Only Manolo knew that the chain saw was in the rear of the shed under a cover," left no doubt in anyone's mind. Two days later, however, Manolo showed up and said he would come to work half a day Saturday. He was all smiles, and not in any stress. He worked that day and promised to return the following Monday to work off the rest of what he owed. He did not show up, nor has he shown up to this day. However, I do believe that we have not yet come to the end of the Manolo Saga. As always in this land, time will tell.

Clear water meets brown water

Food Pura

We live in the country on the side of a volcano at about 6000 feet, and it is lovely and cool. On clear days we can see the Pacific Ocean from our patio. And in January – why that is the month for earthquakes I don't know – we get the occasional rumble that let's us know the Earth is a living thing. We live one kilometer from a village, five kilometers from a town, ten from a city, and twenty from the capital San Jose, the only big city in the country. We have "learned" the city and the country.

For "things you run out of" we shop at the local *pulperia* - a sort of very tiny general store that seems to be always open. Every village has one or two *pulperias*, and they are really necessary when you are running low on eggs and you want those that are fresh that day! For the weekly food shopping you will want to make the run to the AutoMercado where they seem to have everything American (more expensive); then to Heredia (or Cartago, Alajuela, Escazu, Santa Ana), any city where there is one of the dozen HiperMas or MasYMenos stores (cheaper).

When I first went in a HyperMas store I said "Just like a Wal-Mart!" (And, of course, two months ago Wal-Mart bought controlling interest in the 'Grupo' that owns 200 plus stores throughout Central America, including HyperMas). And there are exotic foods! A sampling would be: mango tierno, limon duke, mansahilla, quanabana, guayaba china, kiwi, purple cauliflower, chayote, ayote, yucca, nampi, tiguisque, name, raiz de choyote, papaya, noni, and five different kinds of bananas!

However, for some really specialty items there is no hope

for it but to drive into San Jose. I have never met a person who enjoyed driving into San Jose. More about the big city later on.

Toni is a great cook, and she finds the vegetables and fruits here are exceptional. You don't know what it's like to eat vegetables that have never been sprayed by pesticides, and have never had preservatives sprayed or injected. Carrots taste sweet; broccoli, even cauliflower actually taste good! You will also find you will do more shopping if you buy local foods because they will only keep a few days in the fridge – no preservatives, remember?

There is talk that some of the larger farms in the country are starting to use insecticides and probably spraying too much, so we will be rinsing our vegetables when we get them home. Precaution. Last year an article in the *Tico Times* – the English language weekly that most expats read devotedly (comes out every Friday) – told of a recent lawsuit in neighboring Nicaragua wherein three U.S. companies – Shell Chemical, Dole, and Standard Fruit – lost a suit filed by banana plantation laborers who were sickened by pesticides. (The legal-eagles here have learned something from the U.S. class action suit lawyers). The award was $82.9 million!

There are some food "drawbacks," to be sure, and meat is one of them. CR does have major beef raising areas in the northwest and the southeast sections of the country but it seems to me that grass-fed cattle do not provide as tender meat as does corn-fed stock. The meat on display in stores has little of the fat marbling that usually means tender beef. The only cut of meat that approaches "tender" is *lomita* – exactly that word – which is the tenderloin of the finest quality beef, and every now and then we find a really tender piece of *lomita*. We have tried a regular cut of beef for hamburgers and it is always tough to eat – hamburger! A restaurant owner friend told us that the best meat is always exported. Expats are always discussing where one can find a tender cut of beef. Also, fine cuts of lamb are difficult to find since most of the restaurants get the rib chops, so the shoulder chops are what are available in the meat counter. Veal is very difficult to find, but tender pork is always available. Chicken – *pollo* (pronounced *poyo*) – is the staple meat diet of CR. Fish and most seafood is also readily available. The best fish – low cost and delicious – is talapia – although dorado or corvina could take a close second. Also, you can always find octopus and great shrimp, from the tiny bay to the X-tra Large Tiger Shrimp. Some of it is fresh from the shore, and some is frozen, and you really have to question the clerk at the counter. He will, of course, tell you "everything was caught this morning," so you will have to smell the fish or shrimp you are thinking of buying – really – smell it right there. And question him again. He may relent, look around, and say in a sotto voice, "*Si, pero ….*" and proceed to say in Spanish that "the fish is a few days old and you can cook it tonight but not tomorrow." Scallops are also available, but you won't see much lobster except at the beach.

There really aren't many foods I had in the U.S. that I miss here. We eat pretty much the same; everything is just fresher and tastes better. There are little things you will learn such as having the bacon you buy cut very thin from the slab – it will be more chewy than you are used to, so have it cut thin. As for eggs, the local ones are always within a few days of immediate! They sell them by the kilo (2.2 lbs) or parts of a kilo, or they come packaged in lots of ten and fifteen and thirty. They do not sell eggs by the dozen – or anything else I have found. Almost all single item foods are sold as five, ten or fifteen, or by weight. Selling by weight means that they mix large, small and medium eggs to get the exact kilo.

The travel books always have a listing of a few restaurants for all areas and in all price ranges. We have eaten in a few of them around San Jose, and found the books were pretty accurate in their quality assessment and cost. The restaurants range from small and special cuisine (French, Chinese, Italian, and North American, etc.) to eateries offering a large variety of meats and fish for entrees. The appetizers, called "bocas," are usually very good in almost every quality eatery. There are Chinese restaurants everywhere, and the food is really very good and very cheap! The food has a slightly different flavor, and possibly different preparation than American Chinese, but it is excellent all the same.

Now we come to the *soda*. They are everywhere, on many streets in villages, towns, cities, and on roads in the countryside. The word has nothing to do with the English meaning of soda, but simply means it is a small eatery where you get good basic food at very low prices. These little shops can be just one or two tables in what was the garage or front room of a home, or are an adjunct to a store, or can be larger with five or ten tables with a small kitchen in the back. Sometimes the menu is posted on a piece of wood tacked to the wall with no prices. Sometimes there is no menu and the owner tells you what is available.

In a very small two-table *soda* in a village where we stopped for lunch, there was no menu. A man having coffee at the other table responded to Toni's question about having a salad, and he said they were available, so she asked for a simple one when the owner came out of the kitchen to take our order. I ordered a beer along with a simple Tico rice and chicken lunch. A minute later the owner burst out of the kitchen and brushed by us, out the door and disappeared. He returned in five minutes carrying a paper bag. We decided later that he did not have a liquor license, so went and bought the beer at the nearby bar. He was also apparently out of some of the salad ingredients, and bought those for us. Anyway, the salad was gargantuan with everything one could want, and the local beer was cold and delicious. The meal for both of us, with everything, including the tax of 13% was $3.70 *Sodas* are really fine places to have lunch.

In your first few eating ventures you will find it strange to finish your meal and not be approached by a waiter for more water or anything else. The waiters leave people alone once they are served. They won't even come around to see if you want dessert and coffee. You always have to signal them. The same when you are ready for the check. They will not present you with the bill unless you ask for it. Polite. But this country is getting more cosmopolitan in that an "eating guide" has been published by the *Tico Times* that lists over 300 fine restaurants around the country of all different cuisines.

Since I'm a seafood man I do recommend the *mariscos* (seafood restaurants) in this country. They generally have as good a quality as you will find anywhere. These restaurants, large and small, are in every city and in the countryside. You do have to search them out, so look for a *marisco* sign. Also, you should know that restaurants usually have two prices on the menu, one before the 13% national tax is added, and the other with the tax – the one you pay. You may also see charges for a small portion and for a large portion. I suggest you ALWAYS take the small portion because it will be enough for even a large appetite. A 10% tip is added to the 13% but it is the custom in this country to also leave three or four hundred ($.60- $.80) colones on the table with a 5,000 colones ($10.00) bill.

You will also see, all along the roadside – any roadside – in the villages and outside them, tables set up with local fruits and vegetables for sale. Anyone can be an entrepreneur here. After trying out the nearby supermarket for a few months we are now back to buying fruits and vegetables at small stores, fish at the fish market, etc. Fresher vegetables, better taste, and lower cost.

I hate to admit it but if there is any area where the food in this country is less than equal to most other places in the world it is in the desserts. They are certainly not the familiar pastries of home, no pies or other regional U.S. deserts, and not the sumptuous delights of European sweets. Most of the cakes and pastries are less sweet than you are used to – the chocolate, especially, is not the sugar-sweet Hershey of the U.S. The cakes and the more flaky pastries are heavier with less-sweet fillings. The reason is, of course, that for centuries Ticos have gotten along with fruit and sugarcane as their sweet, and they really didn't have much candy and cakes and such. Then America and its soft drink companies came in followed by the fast food giants, and then the candy people, and voila, the population is getting fat and the Health Ministry is concerned! The locals have tried to make good desserts but it just isn't their expertise. When I need a sweet I dip into our stock of excellent dark chocolate bought by the slab for about $10.00 for 2.2 lbs. (kilo)! It is said that this downtown San Jose factory ships to Godiva.

A note about dining out and staying at that delightful small hotel at the lovely scenic resort you were told about. The Minstery De Ecomonia Industria Y Comercia recently complained that 92.5% of the hotels, and 55.3% of the restaurants do not comply with the law to give customers complete pricing information. This means that when you check out of your hotel at any one of the hundreds of lovely tourist destinations the chances are almost certain you will have added charges on the bill of which you were unaware! The price quoted – as we have found out time after time – was just not the actual price. What to do? When you check in repeat the price to the clerk, write it down in front of her, and then complain with smiling restraint when you are charged more at the end. Then, of course, you pay the bill and "eat" the charge. This fact of "over-charging" hits to a hidden side of the Tico. They **will** try to get the best of Americans much of the time. A friend recently said that Ticos, smiling or not, are really figuring how to get the better of you. All expats are foreigners, and all are wealthy!

Finally, I'll say something about shopping "American Style" – which means the PriceMart (owned by Cosco), and Office Depot. There is no difference except American things are more costly here. There is, however, a huge Home Depot type hardware store called EPA (*eepah*), with home supplies, appliances, and about everything else one needs for the home. This huge EPA has everything else you may need at Tico prices.

And, don't forget the malls. Before we came here a friend told us about the "huge and modern malls, just like the U.S.," and indeed they are. Every major area has its large mall, although the best – and most expensive with most American stuff – is the Multiplaza in Escazu, where many Americans live (which means the city has become choked with traffic and people and smog). It is the most expensive place to live in CR. Escazu is soon to have the honor of having the first true Wal-Mart built in CR – the biggest, longest, widest building for a store I have ever seen. They ought to have a moving sidewalk for an old guy to get from one end to the other.

A good village road

Traveling the Roads

Some years ago a popular book titled *Potholes to Paradise*, written by an expatriate, gave the impression that the roads here, all the roads, are full of potholes. From what we have heard, it may have been the case many years ago. Make no mistake, "there are roads aplenty with potholes galore" ... enough for two countries. But the roads are steadily improving as the people gradually find a voice and as tourism becomes the largest contributor to the gross national income. The automobile is relatively new here – only 25 years ago there were not many cars on the then dirt roads – we have seen a three digit license plate still on a 1970's Datsun. So the old people drive very carefully and casually (just poking along), and the kids fly around corners with a death wish. They have no "driving classes" in the school curriculum, no lectures on road courtesy, and no one has to take a driving test! The young teens with a car are like ... young teens with a car.

Traffic accidents are the second leading cause of death in CR. Drinking and driving, reckless driving, lack of any driving courtesy on the highways, and just not obeying the traffic laws such as they are, are the reasons.

And, because of the potholes, no one in his right mind brings a new car here. First, the import duty is the actual cost of the new car, second, a month on these bumpy roads (plus the potholes) and the computers will all go haywire and the car will go to a garage where the mechanic has little or NO knowledge of what makes a 2009 car run. So everyone buys old cars. After five years the import duty shrinks to be reasonably fair. Our first car was a 1986 Jeep that we paid $3,500 for – and that was a fair price here! Our current 1992 Hundai ($6,000) was a relative gem of dependability – it stayed away from the shop for four months. Then its age caught up with it and now it goes in for rehabilitation an average of three days every month or so.

The automobile does play a large role in our lives and most people have older cars – auto repair becomes a line item in the budget. But when you stop and think about it, we really don't have anything pressing us, no job to get to in the morning, and any appointment here can be put off, so it really is no big deal when the car does not work. It will get fixed in due time. And in the meantime we just enjoy being at home reading, a little TV, taking walks, with me writing about car breakdowns and such. A lovely way to live.

Along with the potholes, one of the real contributors to automobile malaise is the way the potholes are repaired. The road crews do not come in, rip up the block, then lay new asphalt or macadam. The pothole repair is patchwork. They dig up around the hole, fill it in, then cover it over with tar. Of course, in time, the whole block is a series of patches over which a car bumps and rattles. That alone is enough to shake loose any errant wire or connection.

Our car is an old diesel and the cost is about what gasoline is now – roughly $3.00 a gallon. I have not yet learned to work with liters instead of gallons but they roughly equate to a quart. (I think). And when you go to a gas station the first time you will get a shock. There is no such thing as self-serve here; everything is full, courteous, smiling service. You don't get out of your car. And if you travel about the country make a note of where the gas stations are on your map (they are identified) because there aren't that many once you leave the Central Valley. There are lots of tire stores around though, and they have low prices you might think aren't real – all the way to really expensive. (How they can sell a new tire for $15.00 I don't know – like some appliances, they might blow out leaving the garage).

One of the anomalies about the road maps here is that all the roads are given the same red line on a map. A small connecting road (that actually could be a boulder-strewn dirt track) that appears to run from one town to another and then connect to a main road will appear exactly the same on the map as the trans-continental highway. That red line you see running over the mountain to the sea that looks like a great shortcut will probably strand you in the middle of nowhere listening to the howler monkeys (that sound exactly like jaguars), if you don't have a 4-wheel drive – or if you do. Some of the back roads in this country are really ferocious. Always ask one who lives here what is the best road to take.

The government, however, has made excellent progress in making the main roads in and around the Central Valley relatively free of the tire and shock busting holes. Also, most of the main roads to the beach areas are much improved. Recently the Government of Taiwan gave some $15 million to construct a new highway in the northern zone between the cities of Cuidad Quesada and San Ramon. Taiwan buys the shark fins harvested by the local fisheries, to the dismay of the conservationists here, and so are playing the money card for influence. They have been burned, however, since the President recently announced CR would henceforth ally itself with China, to the chagrin of Taiwan which has given and loaned this country hundreds of millions of dollars.

Of course, there are many small towns that have been overlooked. The provincial highway departments do not have the funds to keep all the roads in good repair, and in the rural areas, back roads can be really treacherous for miles. Most roads are not free from potholes, but the main roads (which we might identify as federal highways) are usually in pretty good shape. After having been here for over three years I had gotten so used to the holes on the byways that when we traveled to a lovely hot springs resort near Volcan Arenal (the much publicized Arenal Volcano that fires off almost nightly) and found 50 miles of road virtually free of potholes it was something to exclaim about! In contrast, about eight miles of the road leading into Tamarindo – the very popular beach village on the upper Pacific coast – is appalling. I have never driven on such a bad dirt road, and it leads to the second most popular town for tourists in the country! In this large and intransigent bureaucracy there is no rhyme or reason why some roads get fixed and some – even the most important – do not. The business owners in tourist towns regularly visit the provincial headquarters for road repair and get conversation and little else – they always plead "no money." Or they plead that the last administration left them with no money. (Read corruption). As has been paraphrased by someone: "A bureaucracy is a bureaucracy, is a bureaucracy."

When you look out at the beautiful scenery, you must over look, literally look over, the trash – the trash that sprinkles every gutter in every city and roadside in every town and village. Ticos do not have a "Do Not Litter" program, and they do not have a department for cleaning up the roadways and gutters. Where people live there is trash! I have only seen one sign – in the city of Heredia – that said something about keeping the city clean, although there may be others in other communities I have not visited. Ticos just casually throw the candy wrapper, the milk carton, any paper, piece of wood, metal, or anything else they don't want out the window as they drive along. They will throw out some broken appliance, or chair, or sink by leaving it in the ditch next to their home. About 40% of the homes have a high-off-the-ground iron trash bag receptacle just off to the side of their large gate. Those who don't, or businesses, put their bag out the night before. When the plastic trash bag is put out anticipating the truck, and it breaks, or dogs get to it before the trash collector, no one ever cleans up the resultant mess; it just lies there, unsightly, or is washed into the ditches and gutters.

There is trash collection virtually throughout the country – the cities have those huge compactor vehicles that come around reasonably on schedule, the towns and villages make do with a truck. The large municipal dump outside San Jose has been filled to overflowing for two years now, but the government cannot come up with either the money or a place to make a new dump. The wrangling goes on and the old dump keeps overflowing.

No community – village, town, or city – has the resources to have a clean-up force, so the litter just grows. It gets pretty bad during the dry season, and then the rainy season comes and washes some of the trash down the gutters and ditches and into the rivers and eventually into the oceans. The rest just stays there and builds up. The beautiful countryside so lyrically described in the travel books surely has scars!

We had friends who were on a Caribbean cruise call us and asked us to meet them when they got to Puntarenas, the city where there is a cruise ship wharf. It is on the Pacific side, about two hours west of San Jose. We were delighted to drive over and see the town about which we've heard, but never visited. Well, we were embarrassed. I have never seen such trash piled up in every gutter for blocks around the wharf where the huge ships tie up. This is the one place where thousands of tourists are introduced to Costa Rica, and it is a mess. Trash literally piles around the hundred or more tent-stalls that sell to the boat tourists. You would think that someone would realize this is BAD for business and at least sweep in front of his own stall. Our guests were polite enough not to mention the sight, but I was glad to leave the city after we put them back on the boat. Paradise sure has some cleaning up to do!

Yet even with trash lining the roads, many of the cities and the provinces have crews out keeping the roadside weeds down – the motorized weed-whacker and the machete are very big here. Everything is trimmed, except that there is trash strewn all along most ditches! One of these days someone in the "Keep Our Roadside Trimmed Department" will figure out that the trucks that come and pick up the cuttings from the road crews could also rake up the trash – at least on that stretch of road at that time. The old story: if their job is to pick up grass and tree cuttings, nothing else gets picked up!

When you first arrive in CR it would be best if you hire a Tico driver and car and ride around with him for a few days. Driving here is an experience that North Americans should observe from the passenger side before attempting to negotiate the four people walking on the road, the 18 wheeler, the huge Mercedes-Benz bus, the ubiquitous dog-in-the-road, the occasional fruit/vegetable cart, the occasional pothole and the zipping motorcycle that you will never know where it is. Taken individually, there is no problem, but put all of these together on a road that by any account is a narrow blacktop suitable only for two compacts, and the adrenalin does start to flow. You must realize that all of them together is really what you get every time you get behind the wheel!

It is natural that what makes this country so lovely is the mountain range that goes through the middle of the country from west to east, and that also has the most hilly 180-degree turns, many one-car bridges, and possibly the record for the "most highway-miles-without-a-guard-rail in the world." Every road in the mountains continually twist and turn – a 50 yard stretch of flat is a sight to pull off the road and admire. I counted 25 serious curves from our first home to the small town 5.5 kilometers (three miles) away! But lest you become faint of heart, remember that the usual driving speed on these roads is only around 25 mph so you have time to slow and stop when necessary.

After centuries of using the roads as the only means of passage between villages and towns the local people accept the premise that they have the right of way. They do **not** move off the road when a car is coming. When you are driving on a two-lane blacktop and a car is coming toward you, and there are people walking on your side of the road, you slow down and let the other car pass, then you pull out around the people walking. In the initial first few months we lived here without a car we walked to the local stores and bus stop (a yard-long yellow stripe on the blacktop). Cars have passed me with twelve inches to spare!

When you are driving up or down a hill and come to a narrow bridge (most bridges on other than main roads to the cities are one lane and all have the *ceda* – "yield" – sign on one side or the other), and a bus is coming toward you and you are on a sharp curve immediately before the bridge, and people are walking on one side or the other … well, it is challenging. That is why I suggest you ride as a passenger for a few days with a travel guide before you rent your own car to travel around. Of course, taxis break all the good sense and safe driving rules, so maybe they are not such a good idea.

The buses are great, they go everywhere anyone would want to go, and they are cheap – go from San Jose to a beach on the Pacific – 60 miles – for about $3.00. But they are slow. Take the average speed of 25 mph and then add a bus stopping and starting at each town and several times in between, and you can read half way through *War and Peace* on the way to the shore. Except for the buses on routes between rural villages, the buses are fairly new large Mercedes Benz and very big Volkswagon buses (really), Daewoo, and some other Asian manufacturers, and the ride will be enjoyable.

In using the buses locally, you will find that the front door (and sometimes the back) is always left open, rain or shine. Also, people here are used to the gentile life, and never are in a hurry. So, when a lady pushes the button for her stop, she sits and waits for the bus to come to a complete halt before rising, then ambles slowly down the aisle, perhaps exchanging a word or two with a friend, then carefully negotiates the steps, sometimes pausing to chat a moment with the driver. An impatient North American has the impulse to say "Move it lady!" We know now that "Bus travel is time travel."

You may have read in the travel books that there is an incessant honking of horns. Not so. There is a little horn blowing, but drivers generally use their horns discreetly. You hear the high pitched beep of a foreign car when the driver is pulling out to pass you; you hear a beep if you sit looking at a map when the crossroad is clear; and you will hear a beep and/or a flashing of lights when the oncoming driver is inviting you to make your turn.

But generally there is no indiscriminant use of the horn except in the city when traffic is stalled, and even then only one or two drivers tooting a few times to vent. The story "The Talking Cars of Costa Rica" follows this chapter.

A discussion of traffic would not be complete without mentioning the scores of motorcycles from little Vespas to huge Harleys that will be everywhere you drive. All messengers of business and industry seem to ride almost any two-wheeled vehicle and they drive with an abandon bordering on absolute recklessness. They drive in the on-coming traffic lane when traffic is lined up in the right lanes, zipping back into traffic between cars, on the right shoulder, around trucks, between moving cars and otherwise seeming like non-stop traffic mosquitoes without concern for any vehicle other than their own. We have seen several accidents involving a car and a motorcycle. Most are young kids with a sense of abandon, few driving skills, and certainly no understanding of road courtesy. If there is anything about which I can get irritated in this country it is those damned bikers.

Taxis are also a significant traffic factor – just like any big city, but maybe a bit more of a factor here because the lack of real driving skills, and the same absolute lack of road courtesy – worse than New York or Cairo, Egypt. The official ones are those that are red with a triangular yellow medallion on the side. Many times the cabs in San Jose will try to get away with not using the meter and give you some rapid explanation in Spanish you cannot understand, and then charge you far more than you should have paid. You must always say *"La Maria* (the name of the meter) *por favor,"* and they will turn it on. (Unless they turn around and with tears in their eyes say that the *Maria* is not working today! – then you should get out and into another cab if you are going more than a short distance because you will pay through the nose!) It has happened that the poor driver with the broken *Maria* sits down in his cab and bangs his fist on the meter and lo and behold, it becomes fully operative! He then will run to his projected fare with the good news.

You will also find that a cab in front of a hotel is going to cost more than one you hail on the street – they have the (understandable) idea that people who can stay in hotels can afford to pay more. Also, when you are taking a taxi from one province to another – from San Jose to Heredia – the driver does not have to use his meter, but will charge you what he feels is appropriate – and be sure that "appropriate" means a higher fare when North Americans are in his cab. Before you get in you should tell the driver where you are going by town name, then ask the fare. You will not know if it is inflated or not, so you get in anyway, but it makes you feel responsible by asking.

Once a taxi has a fare he will adopt a maniacal intensity for getting the passenger to the destination with all possible speed. It is as if each person is in the throes of childbirth and is on the way to the hospital. In a really slow line of traffic your driver may simply pull out and drive past everyone, driving on the wrong side of the road with a curve coming up so he can cut in front of a patient person at the head of the line behind a bus. Absolutely insane. And they will always tell you they know exactly where your announced destination is, and then start asking questions of people in the street when they get in the area. You tip as you do in a restaurant – pay the fare then add a few hundred colones tip because he actually got you there alive.

The guide books may say to stay away from "gypsy" cabs – those entrepreneurs who are for hire in every town and village

– but you will find them to be more courteous, friendly, and less expensive than the official taxis. To be sure, you must ask the cost before you get in. These errant entrepreneurs are especially necessary in the rural areas. During a period in 2003 when we were getting settled in our new home we used a gypsy several days a week. Our average cost was about $3.50 per hour, regardless of where we went.

I'm sure that by now you have gotten the idea that the main driving concern is simply the width of the roads. Almost all of the provincial roads from town to town are narrow – built for carts in times past, leveled, then paved over with a four-inch coating of tar. There are few gutters or shoulders. The side of the road might drop off five feet, or be a sheer wall, or have a foot or two of grass shoulder then a sheer drop of 100 feet or more into a lovely jungle of dense tropical forest. So the hazards of the people walking and the potholes are joined by the truck or bus coming towards you. Also, a lot of driving will always be climbing up or down and going around a sharp curve. When an 18-wheeler is coming towards you, and you cannot see how that immense vehicle can possibly get around the narrow twisting curve ahead, much less get past you, it is a fascinating challenge to the driver. The expatriates who live here do take it in stride and without comment. It is just the way the driving is in rural CR.

There are very few expats who will drive at night. The hazards of a possible encounter with a reckless-driving, beered-up teenager, the many people out walking at night in their dark garb, and your trying to find the side of the road without going off the four foot drop when a bus is coming with his high lights on makes it daunting.

Driving in a city such as Heredia or Alajuela or San Jose

presents a different kind of understanding behind the wheel. Many city streets will have square gutters a foot wide and deep, or else there will be no sidewalk – it will disappear for a block or two because the buildings were built right on the edge of the street (or the street was paved right to the building). And you will learn a bad driving habit – at a corner you will have to stick your car out into the on-coming traffic to see if anything is coming, again, because the buildings are constructed right to the edge of the street. I still get apprehensive having to quickly swerve around a car moving out into my lane so it can see me coming. Also, parking has a different twist. In every city, town or village the edge of the road, if there is a gutter or sidewalk, is painted yellow – no parking. But everyone parks by a yellow line or not – wherever there is room is fair game. Space is at such a premium that the police do not ticket for parking by a yellow line or on the wrong side of the road. (That is one thing you have to look out for – when you are trying to determine if the street is one way, remember that everyone may just be parking the wrong way!). And you must remember DO NOT park your car on a side street even for a few hours when you are visiting someone. Car thieves here are notorious and we have heard too many times about a car being stolen right in front of the house. Certainly you should NEVER leave a car parked outside at night!

In every town and city, you will see signs for public parking. These garages or open spaces are a good place to keep your car when you shop. However, because 90% of the garages in the major cities DO NOT comply with the law in providing information on regulations, you may be overcharged.

Another traffic staple is that you will almost always be on a one-way street in any village, town, or city. The roads being narrow the traffic problem is eased (somewhat) with everything being one-way, and there is usually just a small sign on the corner with two arrows pointing the directions. Plus, this being a society of individuals and few regulations, most drivers realize that a stop sign or red light is to regulate traffic, and if there is no traffic coming, there is nothing to regulate, so why stop? Logical. Most roads in cities and most in rural areas do not have a center stripe indicating two lanes. But if there are stripes on the road don't expect Ticos to respect them. If you are driving on your side of a double line, a bus is ahead and there are no cars coming, the chances are the car behind you will simply drive around you and the bus on the wrong side of the road. No-car-coming is the key (a curve just makes it more interesting). Individual judgment. My driving rule for survival: "Drive Aggressively Defensive."

Now we come to the fun part of being a road warrior here: your "destination." You should estimate your travel time, then double it! With no street names, no street signs, and no house numbers, how can you find where you are going? There are rules:

• In most of the towns the roads are one-way north and south
  and east and west

• All directions to you will be given by compass points, by meters,
  and by the church that is in the center of every
  community, large or small. And the church always faces
  to the East!

• Your directions will be: "You will be going north into town.
  When you come to the church go past it and turn at the
  first right East. Go 200 meters, then turn North at a

hardware store and go 100 meters, turn East down a dirt road to the first road South on your right at a large pine tree. We are the second black iron gate on the left past the wood bridge." Piece of cake.

In San Jose directions are given by *avenidas* (avenues) and *calles* (streets) north/south, east/west, and, of course, locating a building by other buildings nearby. Everything is one-way and the maps will show this. However, it is really probable that some one-ways **will have been reversed** if your map is more than six months old!

It does appear, however, that the government is going to initiate a program to name every street and number every house within the next ten years. How this will be done I couldn't guess – some older areas are a crazy patch of alleys and shacks and homes and mansions and fields that are just everywhere. But I am sure that eventually this will be accomplished and the country will be better for it. It will save much time driving around looking for "the block where the dog burned up last year" (one of our recent directions).

I won't say much about driving in the big city San Jose, and I expect you will experience it in a small way when you get here, so you will be forewarned. Suffice it to say that the city is jam-packed with people, the car and bus traffic is horrendous, the smoke and din awful, and it will take you forever to drive anywhere. Estimate your travel time, then triple it. We live twenty kilometers (around fourteen miles) from downtown San Jose and we always allow a minimum of 1:00 – 1:30 hours for a meeting in center city, depending on the time of day.

Remember, the average Tico driver is new to the automobile

– a relatively few decades. In twenty years the number of cars on the street has increased 500% while the amount of road has increased 1%! Therein lies the problem. The congestion, plus few driving skills, plus no learned courtesy, have made CR the most dangerous country in North and South America, with the **fourth highest traffic accident rate in the world in 2005 – and the rate is going up!** Of course, the courts have not caught up with this modern weapon, and here they call a vehicular death caused by a drunk driver "involuntary." The young driver learned to drive from his peers – something like the blind teaching the blind. A well-known expat author recommended using a bicycle but admits it is so difficult to ride a bike on these roads that he walks.

There are few driving schools, and as I mentioned earlier there is no driving test to get a driver's license! When you want one, simply go to the MOPA (stands for a lengthy title that means "auto license department") and get in line. Also, the young man getting a license is a Latin = *machismo*. Add to this that there are few regulations governing driving. The Tico uses the car as an extension of himself.

Drivers are different in the city than in the country – the Tico changes into a more aggressive individual than when he or she (more women are driving these times) is in the smaller towns or the country. In the city Ticos drive as pure individuals. They drive to get ahead, to "beat the traffic," and believe it or not, they drive so as to not waste time! They will U-turn around at a stalled line and seek another route faster than any urban society I've ever lived in. They are all on the way to the hospital! A Tico will pass on the right side of you if there is the barest car width; he will always take the easiest way through congestion trying to squeeze out around cars, bump through a non-manned road repair site to pass a half-dozen cars, then jockey aggressively to get in line when the road goes from three lanes to one; he will swing out and drive in the opposite lane if there are no cars coming then pull in farther up the line and force someone to give way and let him in line. It is all done with a politeness, no one even gestures at another, there is no road rage, it is just the way driving is done here and it is acceptable. It does alert the senses of a North American because it is just not his way of decent, or even safe, driving.

Finally, I must forewarn you, virtually everyone who drives here gets into an accident eventually. Most are small fender-benders or bumper-to-bumper things, but accidents, nonetheless. And they require a certain knowledge about how to handle them. In the first place, who hits whom is important here, with the Napoleonic code that says one is guilty until proven innocent. To determine that, the law states that no car in an accident can be moved until the police come and see everything and give you permission to move it. As a result, traffic can be slowed or held up for hours. So if you hit someone in a fender-bender, the best thing to do is settle it right there, with cash. Ticos are used to dealing this way and it is appropriate to say "I will give you 20,000 colones ($40.00) to settle this." You never say "It was my fault" even if your negligence was blatant – if you do, the Tico driver could collapse on the roadside complaining of head injuries resulting from the slight fender dent. Most of the time he will negotiate and you might have to come up a little, but it will be settled.

Sometimes you have to get an understanding of what the damage is worth. Sometimes the Tico (it's always a Tico involved) will call his garage (everyone has a friend who owns a garage) and get the damages right there (or pretend to). Of course, it will be inflated since you are a *Gringo* so you pull the "I know it's worth

60 thousand, but all I have is 50 thousand" and try to settle it then and there. Not knowing anything about body repair costs here I suggest you offer 20 or 30 thousand colones ($40-$60) for a banged-in fender. A dented bumper, a smashed headlight or taillight should be around the same. Chances are the money will look good to a hardworking Tico who will repair the fender himself (or forget about the dent), plus the fact that he knows what it will be like if the police come and make this a "federal case."

Here's what happens when the police get involved: It will never be more than one officer unless you have a really serious situation. (They don't have enough policemen here to converge ten squad cars to the scene of a fender-bender, as they do in the States). The officer looks everything over and writes the situation down as he sees it. Remember, the other guy is probably a Tico and he is telling the cop that you deliberately drove into him and that he barely got away with his life. If the accident is more serious and one of the cars has to be towed, the process becomes more detailed. (If you are towed make sure you get the cost of the towing with the cop present or you will pay through the nose!). You might take down the cop's name and badge number in front of the tow truck operator. It won't do any good, but it will make you feel better.

The cop on the scene will give you a ticket and tell you to file your report in ten days to such and such an agency in San Jose. There, you will meet with an accident assessor who will take down your statement. So, you take your written version of the accident (in Spanish) and a schematic drawing of the cars – who was going where – with you to the official building and sit down with a serious person who will write it all down as you tell him or her, and then take your written statement. That's it. If you don't speak with fluency, take a translator with you! The written report then goes to a judge somewhere, who, **in about a year(!)**, will send you his decision and what the fine or cost will be. I cannot tell you what happens next because the only one I was involved in (my fault, but he hit me!) was over sixteen months ago and so far I've heard nothing. Sooner or later, however, the bureaucracy will cough and I will hear about it.

Remember that in this country if you are driving 15 miles an hour in traffic, are driving up a street in the outside left lane of a three lane street, and some in-a-hurry joker on your right decides to cut across in front of you and make a left turn into a side street and you hit him it is your fault! Who hits whom is very important. That he was driving stupidly and almost guaranteeing he would get hit is unimportant. You hit him, you pay.

The Talking Cars of Costa Rica

I suspect that Costa Rica has one of the more unique systems in the world for negotiating automobile traffic. Over my octogenarian years I have driven in traffic in twenty or more countries around the world, and it is hardly a revelation that in most cities the automobile horns, indeed the machines themselves, are used aggressively, a reflection of the human attitude.

But each culture does have its own approach to driving in traffic. In Rome the cacophony is dinning as everyone maintains a continual staccato that shouts "movemovemovemove." In Cairo there is also a continual blast but without the urgency, Cairo drivers knowing they can always negotiate a camel-clogged roadway by driving on the sidewalk. In London everyone seems to drive more discreetly, and with only an occasional beep of the higher pitched horns that seem to say "Pardon, sir," the British being a culture that laid the mantle of genteel reserve on the automobile. In Paris the horns are used in the manner of the wedge on the front of a snowplow as they attempt to clear the road, with a continual blast, the many tones blending into an impossibly discordant harmony.

New York has a different make-up, it being 98% taxicabs with multi-colored busses sprinkled among the yellow. The rare private vehicle one sees among the cabs jammed four-abreast, bumper-to-bumper, is always seeking an escape into the cavern of a garage, not daring to add to the single continuing blare that overlays the city virtually from dawn 'till late night. New York taxi drivers lean on their horns from habit, giving a sustained, protesting call, knowing there is nothing that can be done to ease the total gridlock.

But in Costa Rica, a land of gentle people, there is a completely different understanding of the purpose of the horn on an automobile. Having had this mode of transportation in significant numbers in only the past twenty or so years, Costa Ricans adapted its use in the manner of their culture – just as humans have a voice, so does the automobile, and it is given its place in society. It is understood that the horn is the part of the car that is used to communicate. Costa Ricans drive more slowly out of necessity – the roads outside the cities are narrow, twisting, curving, hilly blacktops. And the traffic in cities designed for the oxcart is intense, and like many others, jammed to the point of ridiculous. In such an environment, just as humans get irritated on occasion, so will one sometimes hear the strident beep of a horn in traffic that has been stalled for several minutes for no apparent reason. One horn will toot, then perhaps another will add its voice, but rarely will more than just a few of the cars in a jam push on the horn simultaneously, the other automobiles knowing that a protest has been made and there is no point in adding to the noise. The jam clears up in due time, and one drives on. This forbearance is part of the nature of people here. Time is relative, and all know there will always be enough of it.

This relaxed attitude is endemic in the culture. Just so, the automobile horns have become integrated into this understanding and so are used as communication, as talking points, like nowhere else in the world. When you are creeping along in a solid line of traffic and you see a driver coming from a side road needing to enter the line, you will hear one toot from the car as a question – "Toot *(May I enter your lane)*?" You respond with two sharp taps on the horn "*Yes, pull in front of me.*" The other driver slides neatly into the lane ahead of you and gives you one toot: "*Thanks.*"

Your courtesy is returned when you are climbing up a narrow hill behind a laboring truck and want to pass. You toot twice telling him you are there and the truck pulls over at the first wide spot to let you by. You toot once "*Thank you,*" and he replies with a toot: "*My pleasure.*" The same politeness is observed throughout the country on most of the roads, which are always blacktop, without center or side stripes, and in many places too narrow for two cars to pass. It is understood that the car going downhill pulls over in the first available wide area to let the car coming up the hill have the passage. It toots a "*Thank you*" as it slides past. The one toot reply says "*Con mucho gusto*" (with much pleasure).

When you are in a line of cars and trucks going up the ubiquitous hill and see no opposing traffic, but the car ahead is too close to the large vehicle to see ahead, you give a short toot saying "*It's okay to pass, nothing coming.*" He will pull out, toot twice, both as a thank you and to tell the truck that cars are going to pass, and in a trice all the vehicles behind the truck have pulled around and sped away.

Many times, when traffic is just idling along through a village and pedestrians are waiting to cross the street, a car will stop, toot once to the pedestrians who look at the driver who smiles and nods, they cross with smiles and nods, and the car drives on.

The horn is used to signal direction, as well. If a car in a line of traffic wants to pull out, cross the oncoming traffic and turn into a side street, the driver, turn signal on, will look at the on-coming driver and toot once, then move his car a foot or so into the middle of the road. The driver of the on-coming car slows, toots twice to say *"Okay, cross, I'll wait,"* the car in the line pulls across the traffic. None of the stopped cars behind in either line blows a horn in impatience since all know this is the way traffic is negotiated – two cars talking to each other, asking questions, getting answers, and resolving a driving situation with civilized ease.

In this pedestrian country it is acknowledged that a car will not toot at those walking in the road, many times three abreast on a narrow two-lane blacktop. People have no horn to talk with and so are always given the right of way in all circumstances. If in fact a strolling group of young people does move to the side as the car slowly moves around them, the horn sounds a thank you toot. Also, there is no pecking order here. Automobiles will slow behind strollers, a bus will pull aside for a compact coming up a hill, a garbage truck, normally the ruler of all traffic lanes, will yield politely for the car needing passage, giving a *"You're welcome"* toot in response.

Costa Rica is one place in the world where the automobile horn has found a tranquil place in a tranquil culture.

Renters or Buyers?

Getting into a home here is really tricky and one must know the facts. Americans will consider the customs here "quaint" when renting a house.

There are three kinds of rentals here: (1) unfurnished, (2), partly furnished, and (3), furnished. Be advised !

No. 1 means that the house is really bare – no stove, refrigerator, certainly no dishwasher, probably no water heater, and no furniture of any kind. And if they don't have built-in closets (probably not) there will be no wardrobes.

No. 2 means that you get the refrigerator (10-12 cu.ft., used), stove (4 burner, used), and the water heater (20 gal. tank, used), nothing else.

No. 3, ah, what you need before deciding on buying or renting. You will get all from Door Number Two above, plus a couch, overstuffed chair, a dining room table with two chairs, a bed and wardrobe in each bedroom, a small table or two with lamps, sometimes the dishes and linens are provided – at two items of each for everything. A cheap coffee maker, a large and small pot and pan, and the odd large serving spoon round out the furnishings. No window coverings.

There is no question that when a person rents a completely furnished house it will only cost him several thousand dollars to furnish it to actually live in – depending how many appliances you will replace and buy – do you really want to have enough hot water for two showers in the morning? ... and don't you want a larger refrigerator to entertain more than a couple at a time?

Get a lease before you move in – the owner will usually not allow you to move in without it. The renter in CR has the law all his way – easy in, awfully hard to get him out. And pay your rent in U.S. dollars because of a law that says the owner can not increase your rent for three years (the usual term of a lease) when you pay in dollars, and the lease is automatically renewed unless the owner gives you three months written notice. I can't go into all the ramifications of renting – you can get that from talking with expats and the local attorneys when you come. BUT, be awfully careful about the attorney you use – get one highly recommended by a trusted American, and then check him out if you can. The ARCR – the English speaking organization in San Jose that assists newcomers to this country – provides lawyers who won't overcharge and who seem to know their business. Always hire an attorney who is also a Notary Public. N.P.'s are actually more important and in this country and have more authority than an attorney.

Buying a house here is when it gets really tricky. Because of the extraordinary boom in housing, the spurious developers have come out of the woodwork. There are many "developers" who make claims about having lots of developments for sale, and put lovely scenic views on the internet, that just are not true. Once having gotten deposits and "sold" some property, they will simply change corporate names and do the scam all over again. One of the problems is that anyone can sell real estate here – just hang out a shingle. There is no license or regulation, anyone can sell you anything, and many do. Contact someone who has been recommended to you by an expatriate here who knows the business. This problem exists especially at the beach communities.

A scam realtor will put up grand pictures on the internet and seem as solid as a rock, but be as crooked as the insect underneath it. One of the "legit" scams is for a developer to buy up the mountain behind a lovely beach and say nothing about the fact that the rip tides are so deadly no one ever swims there. As an expat put it in a letter to the editor in the *A.M.Costa Rica* on-line newspaper, "... I used to rationalize the extreme dishonesty, greed, selfishness, and lack of commitment to anything more than a bigger, better deal ..." He announced his intention to leave CR after seven years of frustration.

As to places to live – rent or buy – there is the Central Valley Area, and then there is every place else! You can lump all other places in Costa Rica, aside from the beaches and the Central Valley, as rural and individual, and there are many, many lovely places. The usual preferences break down like this:

Escazu: A relatively small community south and west of San Jose. Very popular with North Americans who have made it a crowded and over-priced place to live. Prices are from 25 – 35% higher here than anywhere else in the country, aside from some special enclaves of super-rich North Americans. A 2000 sq.ft. condo will cost around $250,000. Add around $50,000 to the cost of any house if it is in Escazu. This town has smog, dense traffic and high prices of food, furnishings, and everything else, with fair climate.

Santa Ana: A few miles to the west of Escazu is this slightly larger community that is rapidly getting up there in price as Escazu fills up. At this time homes sell for about 20% less than its rich neighbor. The climate is, to me, much warmer, however. (There are at least ten different climates in CR, and even more when considering the individual towns).

Alajuela: This third largest city in the country, west and north of San Jose, has homes in all price ranges and is closer to the airport. On average houses will run 20% less than Escazu and Santa Ana. It is a bustling but nice place to live. The climate is a nice average-to-warmer.

Heredia: North of San Jose, the fourth largest city, with about 100,000 population is older and cooler. The smaller communities – **Barva, San Rafael, San Isidro, Santa Domingo, Santa Barbara** – have lovely homes scattered throughout the area ranging in price from $100,000 to $2,000,000. The small communities are delightful, and the living is easier, the weather cooler. In the higher altitudes (5000 – 6000 ft.) north of San Rafael you get an afternoon mist (*pelo de gato* – hair of the cat) almost every day that keeps everything green. The nights are really cool – high 50's low 60's.

Grecia, Atenas, & San Ramon: Three lovely, small communities west of San Jose that have a wonderful climate. Grecia is one of the cleanest and well-managed cities I have seen or heard of in the country. San Ramon (west) is getting very popular (Some international study said it has the best climate in the entire world!), and Atenas (southwest of San Jose) are becoming more popular as they are farther out – an hour plus to the big city – which is desirable.

Pavas, **Rohrmoser**: The communities on the west side of San Jose that are a little higher priced and more desirable places to live. These are older communities, have wider streets, and are close to the big city. The U.S. Embassy is in Pavas.

Cartago: the second largest city in CR is to the east of San Jose. A large, flat bustling city, it is hotter than most areas around San Jose.

Now, consider security in this peaceful country – a must. You will have noticed that every house, every single one, from the meanest to the mansion, has an iron fence, an iron gate, and bars on the windows. There is a reason. Crime! Observe the fencing, the gates, the door locks (double, with dead bolts), and the window bars, and the area. If there are any English speakers around, ask about the crimes, etc. in that neighborhood (There will be crime in that neighborhood although the local realtor will tell you there is none). You also should have an alarm system that includes motion as well as sound, and it should be tied to the police if possible. The ADT alarm company seems to do a lot of business here. I suggest all this because if you are from the U.S., all Ticos think all *Norte Americanos* have a portion of Fort Knox under the bed. Even in a "gated community" you must be cautious.

As a side note you will also notice the "iron baskets" about four feet off the ground outside many gates in the towns. These are the trash bag receptacles that keep the dogs from getting to the trash and scattering it all over the street.

And consider getting a dog. There is a reason why there are ten billion or so dogs in CR. Ticos look upon our four-footed friends as "alarm systems with a heartbeat." Even the poorest homes have their dogs. It is only necessary that the dog bark. You don't need a Doberman that will silently go for the throat; get a little yapper who will wake you in the middle of the night – and that will let the intruder know you are reaching for the phone to call the police. If you live in the country you will get used to the dogs barking and the cocks crowing early in the morning.

One final admonition: make very sure that a telephone comes with the house! If you are renting, the previous renter may have taken it with him and **the telephone number stays with the phone**!! If you are buying a new house, it will not have a telephone, and you must apply for one. Here is where the problem comes in. Telephones are very difficult to get here because there are not enough lines installed to handle the traffic. We have heard of people who have waited for two years and still cannot get one. When you are negotiating a lease or a price and you ask about the phone and the owner says "Oh, we have checked and you can get a telephone here as soon as you apply." That's a lot of garbage. **Do not believe it**. Ask him if he will put in the lease that you pay no rent until a phone is installed. He won't, and then you know that the phone will be a problem, not to mention a line for your computer. Don't even think of high speed internet. Also, ask if RACSA – the internet company – has service to the house, and ask if CABLETICA – the cable television company, has service to the house. If they do not you could be in for a marathon dance of "if and when." It won't be pretty. In this country only 15% of people have access to the internet, and only 25% use the web (there are "internet cafes" in many towns), and about half of those are youngsters.

The English language *Tico Times* newspaper recently carried a story about an expatriate who has waited for two years for a phone and had gotten what he called the "run around." He lives in a lovely town of about 15,000 people near the large city of Heredia. The newspaper investigated and reported on what the ICE – the state-run monopoly that operates the electric and phone system – told them. You would not believe the obfuscation, confusion, and the number of departments involved in just getting the okay to run a telephone line! The whole story is too lengthy to repeat here, but the essence was that when the newspaper started calling ICE it started with one official, then was transferred, one by one, to five different officials in five different departments, none of whom had any answer as to why there were not enough lines in that town, and all of whom referred the caller to someone else! The company finally sent a letter which reads in part: *"With the goal of giving the press office an answer ... we are investigating the progress of the project to expand the network (which has) saturation problems, which is why the network was declared a priority in 2003, 2005, 2006, and still has no solution."* This is a real, honest-to-God bureaucracy! No fooling around here, they **really** do not know what they are doing! As I have remarked elsewhere, **most of the time** the telephone will not be answered when you call ICE because the person at the other end doesn't know what to say. If you do get someone to pick up after the 27th ring, she will immediately transfer you and you will hang on for fifteen minutes and then the line will go dead. There is a grand (in)efficiency of the ICE employee and his or her inability to answer telephones during the working day. Now you have an idea of what you get when you do pursue a problem for months, even years, on end.

You should also know that the telephone always stays in the name of the person who originally took it out. You will get an ICE bill – which will be shoved between the fence posts or jammed in the door – they have their own delivery system – and the name will be someone else's. No problem, just take the bill to the bank (all public utility bills can be paid at the bank) and hand over the money. The name is not important so long as the bill gets paid. A sensible idea, all in all.

Most of the time, and especially when you are considering buying in the country, the builder will tell you about the wildlife that is immediately next to your home – you will be practically living in the fabulous jungle! And that simply will not be so. There won't be any tucans or jaguars enhancing your slice of Paradise. They are disappearing from the landscape.

Of course, one of the real concerns about all the construction going on is for the ecology. There has been an alarming decrease in the population of four species of monkey over the past several years, the jaguar has all but disappeared, and so many of the small animals are no more. Whole bird populations have moved or gone, and it is all accelerating as the enormous boom keeps expanding.

Most people do not know that this country has, or in some cases "had" (the numbers are really rapidly declining), 845 species of birds, 250 classifications of mammals, 1240 species of butterflies, 218 types of reptiles, 1013 different types of fish and even 160 amphibians. Striking! And the country is the world leader in protected areas – 27% of the total land mass of the country is given over to parks or wildlife preserves! I mention this because this extraordinary diversity of wildlife is rapidly – emphasize **rapidly** – declining due to the unbridled growth. One of the "fun" things to do here is the "canopy ride" – swinging through the trees. There has been a proliferation of these rides – jungle entertainment where one swings through the trees on cables at or near treetop height. The idea was originally that one could see the wildlife and forest beauty by quietly moving through the trees from platform station to platform station. The idea took off, and after a number of years the country is loaded (or littered) with these "screamers." Needless to say, no self-respecting wildlife is going to sit around waiting to be seen by yelling tourists that whiz along too fast to see anything anyway. It is now just a kid's thrill ride. The monkeys and parrots have gone elsewhere and their habitat is being rapidly destroyed. A local ecologist told me "Give it 5 years at the most, the wildlife will be gone." Too bad, but that's progress. Isn't it? Yet this is exactly what made Costa Rica so well known throughout the world in the first place – the pristine rain forests, the abundant wild life, the beautiful flowering growth throughout the land … the lush wildness of it all. It has gone from a great many places and is on the way out, for certain, in many others.

A bed for the homeless

Furnishings
and Then Some

When we moved in our first house, friends gave us some advice. "If you want to find a good appliance, try to buy an American brand made in Japan, or at least China!" There are no "Made in the United States" products any more, and very few made in Japan, so China is the best bet. And even then you will probably have a problem because, as a friend here told me, "I think every manufacturer ships his 'seconds' to Central America. None of the appliances last long." We thought it was just a cynical viewpoint.

Well, after a few years here we have a cupboard full of broken appliances – we didn't have the extra money it costs to buy appliances shipped in from America with the high duties on imports. We bought the right U.S. brand, but made in Brazil, or Ecuador, or El Salvador. Wrong. It is the bane of all expatriates – trying to find good appliances that will still be operating a year from now. From hand-held mixers, toasters, blenders, microwaves, and every other small appliance, to washers and dryers, stoves and refrigerators, they will simply quit operating, or they will break down, or the plastic housing will crack, or the handle will break off, or screws will come out, causing the motor to burn up, or the wiring will fray, causing an electrical fire on your counter, plus a dozen more "probables," the day after the warranty runs out. And there are no replacement parts !!!!!!! It will be the greatest stretch of your tolerance driving through the heat and traffic of the Central

Valley, seeking out one store after another, maintaining your polite and friendly attitude as you hold out the damaged item and ask for a new part. Then asking who has it and hearing about a store on the other side of the valley near where a large "cypress" tree burned the year before, and your knowing you must go there and try to find the place even though you know full well you will come up empty if you do get lucky and locate the store. You will be told that there are no parts for the Brazilian-made blender because the manufacturer in Brazil does not ship parts for his product. "They only ship the product. They don't ship parts, *Senor*!"

There are also "special" anomalies in finding the goods you want here. A friend of ours bottles and sells aroma therapy nostrums at weekend markets. She uses large half-gallon glass jars to store her tonics in, and sells them in small brown bottles with plastic tops. The large half-gallon bottles have plastic screw-down lids. A few months ago she found out that two of her three suppliers of the small brown bottles went out of business. She went to the third distributor and the buyer told her they had sold out their inventory in two days, but in a month they will have more: "Do you want to put your name on a list and how many you will need because we will sell out immediately again." (The fact that this distributor is now the only one in the country and will probably sell three times as much as before did not register).

The major problem, however, was that the tops she had to buy somewhere else did not fit the bottles that were imported by the now exclusive supplier! The tops came from another manufacturer somewhere else in the world! (The bottle distributor did not, of course, handle the tops. Not his specialty. He was bottles only!). And you can be sure that those tops from "somewhere" will not be watertight. Nor will the large glass storage bottles have a plastic lid that is watertight. The lids that are given with the bottle sometimes won't even screw on. When this is pointed out to a clerk, she smiles and nods and shrugs. There is no reason for all this – it is simply the way things are done. Someday, perhaps we will be around to witness the change, understanding will shift ever so slightly, and a person who sells bottles will also sell lids that fit.

As a capstone to this story, the lady decided to use a heat gun and plastic shrink wrap around the bottle top as a seal. She found a distributor of shrink wrap appliances in San Jose. Everything went well for an hour the first day until the heat gun went "ZZZaaappp" and quit. She took it back the next day and they replaced it free of charge saying they were sorry and she must have gotten a bad one. (Most unusual, as we have never heard of any other store except PriceMart that would take merchandise back – remember this). A second gun worked for two more days before "ZZZaaappp." This happened two more times, each time the distributor salesman saying he was sorry. Then, after the fourth blow-up, he smilingly admitted that they had this problem with that heat gun before and he suggested he give her credit for the gun (!) and she buy a higher priced one, which she did. It worked for three weeks, then simply stopped heating one morning. So, another trip to the supplier and another higher cost heat gun. She wonders when she will hit the top of the line.

Wood furniture is a big part of manufacturing life here. The small city of Sarchi – about one hour northwest of San Jose – is known as the capital of furniture making; the quality is excellent and the prices are relatively low. Tico wood furniture is really lovely and finely crafted. The sofas and chairs, however, are a different thing. The drawback is that Tico sofas and chairs are small, many times garish, and hugely overstuffed! (I have wondered why Ticos will buy large "overstuffed stuff" to go into the very small rooms that are in most houses). You should consider seeking out an importer of used North American furniture; you can get some great quality couches at relatively low cost. Costa Rican tables can be ornately hand-carved, and the chairs solid enough for a medieval castle. If you spend a little time searching for the item you want, you will find it. Remember, Escazu will have what you want, but will be priced through the roof. (I had a sandwich for lunch at Bagelman's (yes, there are three in CR!) in Escazu and it cost $7.85! Absolutely ridiculous, but there are enough North American expatriates there to pay those prices). Spend the time to drive to Sarchi (where the retail stores get their furniture) – about an hour west of San Jose – and you will get great prices and exactly what you want in tables and chairs, and maybe find an overstuffed item that will suit.

For bedding there is "Jiron" – a large manufacturer of mattresses. They have three qualities of firmness, and seem to be pretty good for a cheap mattress. The prices are around $100 and up. There are other more fancy mattresses – up to $2,000 – and you can find them in any high-end furniture store in any large mall. For all the other items (dishes, silverware, etc.) one needs to furnish a house there is (a) the low end "super markets" such as HyperMas, then the (b) more costly and finer items that can be found in Cemaco and Yamuni, small chains of better quality items, and finally (c) the high end specialty shops in the higher quality malls such as Paseode Flores (Heredia), MultiPlaza (Escazu) and others scattered throughout the Valley. For appliances – mainly Central and South American made – there is Importadora Munqe; and there are a host of small specialty shops that import American appliances, some with very good prices (how they do it is not discussed). Plus, they all carry local and South American brands.

But the seasoned expat here knows to get the *Tico Times* every Friday morning to read the classifieds about who is having an estate or yard sale – someone is leaving to go back to the U.S. or moving to Panama and they are selling their two year old U.S. made and already brought down here refrigerator, washer, and dryer. What a bonanza! The prices will be half a new one, and they will work well. Most probably. If you are new here and wonder how you get a 17 cu. ft. refrigerator from the garage sale to your new place, don't fret, there is always a local "handy man" around with a pickup who will deliver it for $20.00. You do have to tell him to bring a helper because you have a bad back and can't lift a large refrigerator off a truck! Otherwise he will show up and expect you to do the lifting because he delivered – that is what you paid him for, yes? Here you MUST be precise in all your dealings because the Tico interprets everything literally. He will do what you have asked of him. But he does not expect to do what you have not mentioned. And, conversely, he will not tell you something you may need to know if you have not asked him. The Tico is not rude and does not assume you do not know something.

At this point it seems apropos to include my list of how "things" work in this lovely country. With tongue in cheek, there is nonetheless much truth in these pronouncements:

> Note: The assumption is that you will not pay the high import prices for U.S. made products and will shop locally for what is available. Quality tests reveal that items made in Japan are Number One (but hard to find and expensive), China is second best (most of what is around), then Chile, then Brazil, the other South American countries bringing up the rear. The results

below are from actual home tests with some possible exaggeration for emphasis!

Dishwasher – Unless it is brand new it will need repair by the third month of use. If new it will last for an additional 2 – 3 months.

Toaster – Repairs (or junking) will take place within six months. Should you find a rarity and your toaster is still going after that time, it will take longer and longer to toast so by the end of twelve months you need to put in your morning toast before your shower.

Microwave – The average size unit will work from two to six months. However, cracks in the housing will occur at any time from the moment it is put on your counter. These may or may not render the unit useless. With cracks it will also create extraordinary grinding and clacking noises and will flash intermittently.

Blender – A choice of a hundred or so different models is available – they are popular here. A middle price range unit will last a full 3 – 4 months before some tiny cog will break, rendering the whole unit worthless. Tiny cogs are not stocked in Costa Rica.

Food Processor – Add two months to the time-frame of a blender for a middle price-range item. There are no parts for these either.

Floor or Table Fan – This item will probably run through a dry season then die from over-work. It cannot be repaired.

Electric Hand Mixer – A most fragile item. With great care in use it may last a full month. It is designed to spray the food being mixed in a six foot radius. Use behind a glass shield.

Steam Iron – It will work like a dream for at least two weeks and then it will cease creating steam. The iron will get hot, but the regulator will have quit so you will have to learn to judge when it is hot enough, and sometimes pull the plug to cool it down when ironing a delicate fabric – something like heating the old solid iron on the top of the wood stove until you sensed it was hot enough. Use the wet-finger-to-the-bottom technique.

Washer – (Local brand Tico washer/spin-dry). The velocity of the spinner approximates a 737 jet engine and will tear your clothes to shreds. This unit will outlive your youngest child. It must be bolted to the floor or else it will vibrate off any pedestal, across the room and out the door within minutes. The astonishingly loud high whine may kill the dog.

Washer (That looks like a normal one) – this will be an American brand made in Brazil and will last at least three months before breaking down. These can be repaired, as some store somewhere will be able to order parts so your washer will be fixed and operating again within a reasonable number of months.

Dryer – One can only guess at the life-span. It may not work when you get it home. It may run perfectly for a week or a month and then suddenly refuse to heat up. These units come in all sizes, models, and shapes. They can be gas or electric. They cannot be regulated. They cannot be repaired.

Gas Stove – The top burners are a delight to use because they work. The inexplicable oven, however, cannot be controlled. The dials turn counterclockwise, the thermometer will not have any degree of accuracy, there will be no way for you to determine temperature when baking (and this is a brand new one!). You should be an accomplished baker/roaster and so be able to simply "judge" when something is done. In a recent home test the author's wife baked a dish that required 30 minutes at 375 degrees. It took two hours, the thermometer registering 400. Be advised: wear asbestos gloves when baking as the ovens have no insulation and the stove will crisp your hand at a touch.

Hot Water Heater – Most locally made (South America) units are small, and 20 gal. tanks are standard for the small Tico homes. (This size will fill about 1/4 the standard tub – if you are lucky enough to find a home with a bathtub). We recommend always paying the price and buying the U.S. American Standard brand carried here.

Fireplace – Another "if you are lucky enough" item. Most Tico homes do not have them except at 4000 feet altitude and above. However, the technology for designing a non-smoking fireplace (when a one mph breeze is blowing) has not yet reached this country. Every owner will tell you his fireplace is grand. It is, until you use it. During the windy transition months of June and November it is wise to wear a gas mask when roasting chestnuts on an open fire.

Computers – Buy a Japanese brand, or a U.S. brand (which are only made in China). You will have inordinate problems getting a phone line from ICE or in getting a high speed line for your computer – your neighbor will have it but you will be told they will not get to your neighborhood for six months – or in setting up with RACSA (the CR server), and any other government office. You can telephone (if you speak Spanish) to see what is holding up your phone line application but most likely you won't get through. As mentioned earlier, ICE employees rarely answer the telephone and if they do they will tell you to hold on or will transfer you and the line will go dead.

Computer Repair - The computer is of great importance to we expats. There are a *few* good repairmen around the Central Valley. Ask American expats who they use and maybe by the third or fourth try you may find one who knows what he is doing. I do not recommend using an expatriate who, with time on his hands, decided to go into the computer repair business. I have witnessed grown men break down sobbing after they were visited by an expat repairman who trashed their hard drive.

Auto Repair – This topic is so big it needs a book. Everyone's car here is five years old or more, and most couples have two cars (Breakdowns are assumed, so they always have a spare car – one or the other is always in the shop). Suffice it to say that there are approximately 2,915,673 auto mechanics in Costa Rica (give or take 50,000). There are probably six, maybe seven really good ones. Everyone you meet will tell you their mechanic is really good, and then ask you if you know of a good one. You just have to ask around. I can't write about auto repair any more because I begin to tremble uncontrollably.

Home Repairs: Be advised that every single Costa Rican male is an accomplished repairman. He considers himself a plumber, electrician, roofer, auto mechanic, painter, gardener, and construction worker, for starters. There is no piece of equipment made on this Earth that he will admit is beyond his ken (computers being the exception). When you ask your gardener to "Do you know anything about dishwashers?" it will be on the floor in a dozen pieces within five minutes of his pulling out a pair of pliers, and may never be put back together again. We have actually seen ours repaired with a part, a cog, or something else left over, yet the washer runs. We know that sooner or later it will explode mightily some evening after a dinner party. Once we had an electrician arrive at the house with only a pair of tweezers and a bottle of distilled water! Fact. But he repaired the house wiring problem. How, I have no idea.

Telephone: I have mentioned the trauma of a house with no telephone. You should also be aware that the phone will quit working every now and then. If you live in an area that gets lightening strikes afternoons during the rainy season, be assured that your phone will go out more than a few times a month for days at a time. It will take a few days for you to contact ICE (the telephone company – not on the phone – remember, they do not answer telephones), you have to drive to their nearest office building and stand in line for probably only 45 minutes or so (they always have long lines), then a repairman is scheduled for 3 days later (and he might actually show up the day scheduled!). He will fix it easily and you are set 'till next time. We were hit by lightning once – the computer was blown, the tv was trashed, and the phones would not work. A week later everything was fixed (we had to buy a new tv) except that only one of the three phones in the house worked. How can one work and not the other two? All are on the same line and they check out as ok. The phone company says it is the telephone and our electrician says it is the phone line. Beats me, but this is Costa Rica. It only took six days in all for the repair to take place. Luckily we have Skype through the computer so we're always in touch with home folks. How we got Skype capability is fodder for another book, but after five months of very crafty out-maneuvering the government we did it! I should also remind you that when you go to the nearest ICE office to report your problem, take a translator unless you speak really good Spanish. ICE people seem to have their own jargon, and they speak more rapidly than do most Ticos, which is really fast! This means you will hear a stream of five questions strung together with a smile and raised eyebrows. Remember to turn away so she does not see the tears welling up. This just excites her.

Locks: You will need locks for several areas. There are sturdy looking, solid brass, stainless steel hasp "Vale" locks made in China that cost 60% less than the "Yale" locks (get it?). They will work for two weeks and then the key will not turn the mechanism – they have become rusted inside.

Television: This is the one appliance with which we have had good luck!. A 21 inch, no frills set cost $100 and lasted for three years until it was fried by the lightening strike noted above. We bought a new 26 inch, "made in China but assembled in this country so there are parts for it." The box said "Made in China." They should know how to make TV's, right? We bought it at a reasonable price and when installing it we noticed that on the unit was stamped "Made in Korea!" The international trade people are getting really sharp at knowing which country sells and which does not. And in case you are wondering, yes, we do have surge protectors on all computers and appliances. It just seems that the lightening here is more direct, or more powerful, or something, because a lot of people get hit a lot of times.

As a capstone to this appliance list I will mention my wife's "final" declaration: "I will never buy another appliance in this country!" (Said at full voice, an expression of anguish, tears floating just behind the lids). After the second blender had broken down just after the warranty period she decided that the problem was she didn't get a top of the line, top quality unit. Shopping again, we did find U.S. appliances (China made) in a couple of stores we visited, so we invested in a high end Black & Decker "Power Pro," a sleekly styled, black and ominous-appearing machine with eight buttons down the front, and heavy enough to require two people to lift it to the counter. It reeked brute power. With a "Made in China" label I remarked, "At least it's U.S. made!"

Well, the first time she poured some concoction in it and turned it on the Thing gave out a roar that would have done justice to a wounded elephant. I was watching television in the living room and the grinding was so loud I could not hear the TV. Toni shrieked. I ran into the kitchen and saw her standing in front of the blender that had blown the lid off and splattered an orange colored puree over the counter, the window, the floor, and her. "This damned thing ... I pushed the lowest speed button! I think the speeds are reversed!! I... I..." she gave up, the tears trickling down her cheeks in total frustration.

The resultant soup, while not puree, had an exceptional flavor and we got over the matter of the blender with reasonable grace. I mentioned that it certainly did make a loud noise at whatever the setting was and she remarked "I said it before and I'll say it again and I mean it this time: I will NOT buy another appliance in this country!" (When I later tested it with a milkshake I found that it was indeed set at the highest speed, and that all the speeds were the same – high!). Ah … Costa Rica!

General Observations
Government

A subject that could occupy several volumes for this lovely country. This is a "social democracy" with several prominent political parties. The major party recently won a fair number of seats so their man – Arias (Nobel Peace Prize winner 1998, for getting the Central American countries to stop fighting each other in 1988) – got in. He is better than the last one who did little while in office – he was a psychiatrist and he was always asking people how they felt about things. Actually, politics here are not much different than the U.S. Arias promised a year ago to add 1500 police to the force. To date something like 60 have been added. When I read that department heads say there is no money for things, I want to shout "One – stop the corruption! Two, collect the taxes from business!" Whether it is correct or rumor, it is said that there is corruption in every department, and from top to bottom. Actually, at present there are four (count 'em – 4) past presidents under a corruption cloud. Newspapers allege, and departments try to answer, but I have never seen an accounting given after accusations have been made.

It is interesting that this country is now touted as the fastest growing in the world, and we all see the U.S. investment pouring in. *Fortune* magazine recently said that San Jose is the Fifth Best city in Latin America to do business in – not a great endorsement because there are not that many large cities in Latin America. A year ago CR was also named as the 27th best country for investment out of

140 – the U.S. was only 22nd. All this when Standard and Poors gave Costa Rica only a "BB" rating which is **below investment grade**! See the dichotomy here? Humpty Dumpty is going to have a problem!

Also, everyone here cheats on their taxes. I know of businesses that have operated in the city for fifteen years and have never paid a colon (the local currency) in taxes. I started a small business and was told by the lawyer who got me the corporation certificates, "You won't have to pay taxes, just don't report …." and so on. I told him "No, I am going to pay whatever taxes I should" and added something about "my adopted country needing all the money it could get." (My footnote to starting a business in this country is "don't!" – mine lasted six months. You won't believe how the business culture operates).

Only the major department stores and food chains insist on charging you the sales tax on every purchase. We have found that most smaller stores will not charge the sales tax if you pay cash and do not want a receipt. The clerk will always ask "Are you paying in cash?" Buying for a business or for the home, it's the same. I'm guessing that a third of the gross revenue is lost this way. It is part of the culture. The government should mount a campaign saying "If You Are Proud to be a Tico Pay Your Taxes," to change the prevailing apathy.

Although there is actually a "constitutional principal of efficiency and simplicity in administration functions" here, the major complaint about government is the same as in every country, just more severe here – the bureaucratic obfuscation, confusion, ignorance, and anything else you can say about it. The government people, from the lowest ranking clerk to the highest supervisor in a department, don't seem to know anything beyond putting a stamp on the piece of paper that is under their authorization. And, as in most government offices around the world, there always seem to be too many people chatting together, talking on the their cell phones, and otherwise "spinning wheels" – too many employees doing too little work. Only every now and then do you run across a smart young person who makes things happen. The rest could care less about your or anyone else's problem. And worse, they really don't seem to know who to talk to in their own department to get a problem sorted out. They know their job of stamping a paper and nothing more, literally – it is as if the person one step higher up does not exist in their mind so they literally do not know who to call about a problem. Very strange. A management consulting firm would have a field day here. My story about trying to get a driver's license is a case in point.

On the good side, this social democracy is geared for the **people**. The government puts 5% of GNP into education; the laws always favor the people over a business (the opposite of the U.S.); there are unions for the government workers and they are really powerful. When they call a strike the whole country gets behind it. The legal system is based on the Napoleonic code – a man is guilty until proven innocent. When a man can't prove he is innocent, justice is swift – no hanging around for fifteen years of appeals for a murderer. He gets his sentence carried out within only a few months after one obligatory appeal. They don't have the obstacle of "political correctness" in this country.

There is a negative side to this "guilty until proven innocent" code – a judge has to get real evidence that a person appears guilty of the accusation or he will release the prisoner back on the street even though everyone knows the "perp" did it. And, if the District Attorney actually files a complaint against the "perp" then the "statute of limitations" on that particular offense is reduced by half! Since the courts are backed up **for years**, the judge knows he can't put the guy in jail without a trial for years on a small theft crime, so he releases him awaiting his time in court! Then the bad guy goes back on the streets knowing the statute of limitations will run out. The *Tico Times* reported that many cases are lapsing or are in neglect – a prosecutor told a reporter that she is overwhelmed by stolen property cases. The rate of theft – especially those occurring to foreigners, is astonishing. There is a significant shortage of District Attorneys to handle cases, and they are literally all backed up in their case loads for years. There are ONE MILLION cases in court – in a country of four million people! If you get wronged here there is slight chance of your getting justice!

Of major concern for those buying property here is "property fraud" which has increased 700% in the last decade! According to the newspapers, ten gangs have been identified as working with accountants, notaries, and real estate brokers to investigate, then steal the ownership of properties. Independent Notary Public individuals have also been caught signing away your property when you don't even know it! The laws here give extraordinary power to a Notary – more than to an attorney. Fraud has become so epidemic that a private company – Private Property Registry – has been set up to run a second check on the official Registro Nacional. For a reasonable fee each year they will keep tabs on your property registration. A good idea.

There is, however, a very strong legal favoritism for women. You can get fined and even jailed if you are heard cursing a woman – or if your wife accuses you of doing it! (Try to prove you are not guilty!) Striking a woman is a felony and will get you heavy jail time….when your case comes up …if your case comes up.

Police

There is much crime in this country, and there are few police. There **are** police, it's just that the force isn't very large. Thus, the significant increase in crime in the past several years. That plus the fact that they don't have the most modern detection methods – as one of the expat cynics recently put it "The CR police should watch CSI." The small force just seems to be visible as traffic control, and not much else. **This is the first time in 25 years that the country has been training new policemen.** One of the officers overseeing the training remarked to a reporter that "Putting on a uniform and going out into the street is a danger in itself these days." The problem is that CR has only .37 police per 1000 people. The weighted average for 48 countries surveyed was 3 per 1000 people – 8 times more police on average than in CR! One attempt at curbing the breaking-into-a-car theft was to hire and train young "car watchers" to detect possible thieves. It soon became apparent that the watchers themselves became adept at thievery, and when the police were called, the young men "saw nothing." *A.M. Costa Rica* had a Letter to the Editor saying "It is a myth to say that it is relatively safe to travel here. A thief took luggage as it was being unloaded from a tourist bus, got into a waiting taxi, and sped away." Another ploy thieves use is to ride a motorcycle up to a couple walking on the street, pull out a gun and demand cash and jewelry, then hop back on the bike and drive away. The police can do nothing when you tell them.

I have seen local cops in action when a new expat friend was robbed at gun point (guns are becoming more and more prevalent in crimes) and I was reminded of a child taking out his "crime scene set" and dusting the door knob for fingerprints after a dozen people had come into the room. They even questioned me at length because my wife and I were called to come and help the woman after she was robbed. They did not catch the perps even though they had a very limited number of suspects and good tips. The police were in and out of that house for a full week and nothing was accomplished. They always looked serious, as police do. One of the investigating officers tried to get the attractive, affluent, and divorced victim to go to dinner with him.

A recent article in *A.M.Costa Rica* quoted Senor Berrocal, the Minister of Public Safety, who announced new laws to thwart Costa Rica's "growing and grave crime scene." An editorial called it a "rising tide of criminality," and "… highly visible and increasingly embarrassing crime problem … out of control." A letter to the editor said " … the old days of *'pura vida'* are gone, it is dangerous here." Crime is at the appalling stage, and increasing, because there are only 10,000 police throughout the whole country (with 4000 more promised by the year 2010). Today the police do not have enough guns, bullets, uniforms, vests, or vehicles to do their job. It will surprise most to know that **more U.S. passports are stolen in Costa Rica than in any other consular district in the world** – more than all the rest of Central and South America combined! Skulking thieves in Paradise.

In 2005 (apparently the most recent records) crime had a poor record of convictions. Burglary – 3%, Fraud – 4%, Robbery – 4.7%. Thieves have little to fear even if they do get caught! It has been printed that there are around 400 street robberies each month – those that are recorded – in major cities. By October of this year 2007, 2,293 have been recorded. The sad thing is that one will sit all day in a police station filling out papers and answering the same questions over and over again to the same policemen while NOTHING is being done to search for the thieves. And, should they actually be apprehended, by some miracle of Providence, they will probably be booked and then released "awaiting trial!"

While there may be a shortage of policemen, there is no shortage of "Security Guards" – those private police who work for gated communities, who are outside every bank in the country with automatic weapons held at the ready, who work in all larger stores, private companies, and large buildings. There are 30,000 of these strongmen throughout the country who have a single identifying feature – they do not smile at anything or for any reason.

When you are stopped for a traffic violation you may think of the stories you have heard about bribing the cop with a c5,000 note ($10.00) – the assumption being the police are bribable. Probably true, but I wouldn't bet that he won't get angry because a foreigner does it in bad Spanish, and takes you in! There is a place in downtown San Jose where a short one-way street has a very small sign 20 feet up on a telephone pole that says the street is only for buses. I followed a taxi in there (not seeing the sign), and was pulled over as soon as I turned the corner by two cops waiting with their books out. I was told the fine was c7.000 (about $14.00), I paid it, and did not get a receipt, the cop saying it was not necessary! The taxi was not ticketed, I noticed. That beat is a very good money-maker. I will bet the cops are rotated to augment their income.

A hopeful sign for the future is that San Jose has recently contracted for 300 surveillance cameras to be placed around the city in "strategic" locations. Also, all the hotels have met together to coordinate thievery control measures – a good sign!

Firefighters

Another area about which I know little – I've only seen one fire truck in my time here and I have yet to see a fire station. There seem to be few fires in this country. Every now and then we see pictures in the paper of seemingly well-equipped firemen fighting a blaze in San Jose, so we know that there are fire companies around. That there are, or are not many firemen, however, is not the problem. The fact that there are only about 5000 hydrants in the whole country, and only about half of them are operable is the problem. That there are not nearly enough fire hydrants in major cities, and very few outside of major cities, is the reason a fire usually means total destruction. Recently there was a factory fire just outside the city of Alajucla (120,000 pop.). The plant burned to the ground because the nearest water hydrant was about three miles away. Many of the fire hydrants in the Central Valley are useless, and there is no maintenance on the rest – there was **no government department** listed as being responsible for the hydrants! The administration recently appointed the Water Department to be responsible for maintaining the water hydrants. Wow, what a concept! The government admits there is a problem and wants to construct more underground major water lines and have hydrants for every population area, but "there is not any money." My guess is that it will take at least five more years before all the cities and the larger towns have hydrants. The small towns and villages will have to wait longer.

Electric Company

Although it runs the telephone company, the main business of ICE is providing electricity to the country. It seems that even with the predictions three years ago about the expansion throughout this little nation, the growth has caught ICE with its pants down. Perhaps in a government-controlled operation you cannot expect much else. There is comparatively little manufacturing here, so most electricity goes to the consumer, agriculture, and distribution businesses. The major stations produce hydro-electric power – they need water to run the power plants – and one of the largest plants runs off the water in Lake Arenal (near the volcano) which was very low due to the drought this year. In a drought season - and 2006-2007 was one – the electricity goes off a lot! (With the "climate change" the smart people say is upon us there is a real probability that the drought problem will get a lot worse). A few months ago ICE asked the government to allow it to raise the rates (ICE is government-controlled but run by a private organization). The government said "No, you made $60 Million last year and don't need the money." The next day ICE blacked out the whole country for three hours! (*"Don't tell us no, baby!"*) They said they had to conserve energy since production was low. When the howl raised the roofs at the government offices, ICE instituted "rolling blackouts" over the next three days. Of course, there is always someone who will tell anyone who will listen that ICE has reserves stored, and that they are just playing politics. The fact is, however, that this growing country does need more power plants. The Cariblanco hydroelectric plant recently completed in north-central, low population CR, will help the situation by 10%, providing power to 110,000 homes. And there is a new plant to come on-line and be run by a Spanish firm named Central Hydroelectrica La Joya, a few miles from San Jose. It will provide around 3% of the national requirement. For the southern zone there is an approved new loan for $10 million to fund "studies" for a long-delayed hydro plant in that area, and five other plants that will cost $700 million. The largest of these plants will come on line around 2016, if schedules are met, but it is being protested because of a dam that will be built, flooding homes in the area. Plant "planning" has been going on for years, but the government can never agree on the money needed. I have yet to hear what those huge hotels and resorts and towering condo buildings on the Pacific side are going to do when they all get up and running within a few years! Especially since an ad for a mega resort said their water will come from Lake Arenal, which this year didn't have the water to keep the electric plant it supplies operating full time! This year there was a drought and if it continues for a few more years – when the huge resorts, condo buildings, and apartments are ready for occupancy – there won't be water for electricity, much less to pipe and truck around the country. There are many government heads in the sand, and there are many smiling heads of builders selling high-end condos to the wealthy for occupancy in a few years!

The power plants now in the idea stage will take five to ten years to get into production, and they will probably do little more than meet the current needs, according to some knowledgeable engineers. They have taken into account the normal growth of 7% to 10% a year, but I bet they still have not considered the mega stuff that is going up in several areas. The power company is now having controlled sporadic blackouts for "maintenance." And now that CAFTA is approved, and U.S. money starts building manufacturing plants because of the cheap labor and proximity to the U.S., where is the power and water going to come from? There isn't any planning. *Nada*. The houses of government here do not look ahead to next year, much less five years! And when they do, some faction in the congress – the environmentalists, the liberals, the conservatives, the socialists, or some little group on the fringe that can stopper everything will jam it all up for a year. But I don't have a house or business to worry about, I rent, so I just take out a book when the TV goes off. I have the best Coleman lantern made! (One of the few things left that are "Made in the U.S." – I think).

There are other really huge problems with the infrastructure. Because of a major bridge disaster in the U.S. (in Minnesota), the bridges of CR came under the *Tico Times'* scrutiny. Many, many of them were built eighty years ago when CR was a horseback and oxen nation. Many bridges were built with wood. We take our stateside visitors to see a lovely waterfall and point out the bridge near it that just collapsed one day as a chicken truck was driving over. The remains of the former bridge are still lying under the new steel one that replaced it. Not one chicken was lost! The Japanese (JICA) recently finished a two-year study of the country's bridges and determined that the 1,330 bridges of the national highways suffer from **severe deterioration**. The government admits that most of the bridges are fifty or more years old, but the Public Works and Transport Department of the government made a typical politician's statement: "Most of the bridges are in good condition – they just need updating." The newspaper was unable to get a copy of the Japanese report. CR has 6,800 bridges in all, but 5,500 of those are in municipalities, **which were not even considered in the study**. My friends, when you drive to

Manuel Antonio, and you have to drive over a couple of those bridges that are **on the main road to the most popular tourist location in the country**, you will know what "scary driving" is!

The Arts

Music: A peaceful society usually supports the arts, and for such a small country CR has an excellent handle on this. The symphony orchestra is a case in point. It is small – just 60 pieces – but I have seldom had the pleasure of hearing a finer orchestra, large or small. The conductor is Japanese, and they have quality guest conductors from the U.S. and Europe from time to time. They vary the program so that most tastes are accommodated, rarely putting Mozart with Mahler, but when they do they make it work! The Teatro Nacional was built back in 1897 because the famous diva Adelina Patti offered to come and sing. She did, and they presented Gounod's *Faust* to much acclaim. The theater is ornate and small, the seating being only around a thousand, with excellent acoustics, and it is delightfully reminiscent of the fine opera houses of Europe. Three tiers of balconies overhang the gently sloping orchestra floor, emphasizing the intimacy of the design. They also feature pop solo artists, jazz festivals, big bands of the '40's, and cater to all musical tastes. You will enjoy the sound.

There are also several different musical groups that present music of different cultures from time to time, and the universities also present their symphonies in various venues throughout the Central Valley.

Theater: The dramatic arts are well represented in CR. The English speaking amateur "Little Theater Group" has been around for many years in the home of an Escazu patron who remodeled her ground floor to seat forty. The stage is small, but the quality of theater is quite good, given that all they have to work with are sets with few drops, scene changes, and similar theatrical requirements that help us in "suspending belief." There are also thirteen Spanish language theaters throughout the Central Valley offering everything from musicals to the avant guarde to Chekov. Even Shakespeare can be found in visiting ensembles from England and the U.S. There is a Eugene O'Neill Theater in San Jose and this week a troupe from the State University of New York-Buffalo is presenting a musical. Something happening all the time!

Visual Arts: The museums are high quality and worth a visit! There is the National Museum of Culture, the Gold Museum, the Jade Museum, and the Museum of Art. On the private side, on one weekend in April, 2007 there were 19 art exhibitions, openings and shows throughout the Central Valley, and probably double that throughout the rest of the country. There are hundreds of galleries throughout the county, many times coupled with a frame shop, but nonetheless, an art gallery. The quality is just as varying here as in the U.S., with the preponderance of the paintings having a "Costa Rican" emphasis, or a Latin theme. The usual painting seen in a gallery has bright colors and features florals, birds and rural life. The finer galleries, with prices that can be in the thousands, many times feature more famous Mexican, Peruvian, and Argentinean artists. But you can find about any kind of painting you want. I firmly expect that soon there will be a gallery featuring only North

American artists because there are so many really good artists living here now.

Sculpture is also available in many mediums – wood, bronze, iron, plaster and more. The ubiquitous free-shape wood bowls that are sold in most of the "gift shops" (read tourist) in hotels are done by fine artists making a living. Their abstract sculptures sell for thousands here. There are few glass works, or the more esoteric art mediums. If you have a talent, the market is open for you.

Dance: There is a National Dance Company and a half dozen or so small dance companies throughout the country. While these dot the Central Valley, there are more in the populated beach resorts that are basically schools, and offer limited recitals. However, every now and then a known foreign company travels to CR and performs for a week in San Jose. The smaller companies offer recitals in ballet, folk dance, modern jazz, hip hop and more throughout the season. And there are classes for about every kind of dance.

You might have figured out – and correctly – that I believe that a country is remembered for the quality of its education and its arts. This little country has more than one would expect, and the government supports most of it. Perhaps there is the view that if everyone is dancing there is little need for a policeman.

The Driver's License

As in all countries, obtaining or renewing a driver's license is a tedious and sometimes complicated procedure. That it need not be so is a given. But it does seem that this is the one government agency, in any country, where the petty bureaucrat can exert his or her authority and cause all measure of obfuscation and confusion. Patience is the key requirement to success.

Thus it was when we went to get our driver's license from the MOPT, the Departmente of something that, in Spanish, means motor vehicle regulations including the license bureau. It is in the capital city of San Jose. Our expatriate friends gave us suggestions such as "Go early, there may be long lines," and "Make sure you have all your papers and get a medical examination right there before you go in." We were accompanied by our friend Melanie, a tall, blonde forty-year-old who is a ten year U.S. expatriate, perfectly fluent in Spanish. She was getting her license renewed and knew the drill.

The MOPT is in a somewhat run-down section of the city, as seems to be the case with Departments of Transportation in cities in any country. Our driver/guide Melanie did not remember the exact location (and finding your way about San Jose even with a described location is a challenge) so we parked the car in the middle of the city and took a taxi. It delivered us to the front steps of a block square, unadorned two-story, gray cement building. As we stepped out of the taxi I noticed three sidewalk tents signs advertising Physician Examination. Unpainted storefront doctor's offices to meet the state requirements for medical approval before one can be deemed safe to drive. Melanie said we might as well go to the doctor she had used two years before. She remembered that his "office" was in a public parking lot.

I looked down the street and saw a rather large sign announcing a *medico*, and saw it was in a parking lot. Our doctor. A young man was standing in the street calling out *"Examen, 3000 colones, examen, 3000 colones"* (about $6.00), a shill for the esteemed physician.

Entering the parking lot we saw a small metal tent sign *"Medico"* next to an open door in a low cement block building. We entered a room about 8 feet wide and 15 feet long of unpainted cement block walls where hung three framed diplomas from universities in Costa Rica; a bare tin roof covered the room; the floor was unpainted cement. The doctor's desk at the rear held a black telephone and two worn volumes propped up by a stone and a brick. The rest of the desk held a small stack of forms, two pens, and a tiny hand-calculator. A straight-backed chair was placed next to the desk. A row of four attached plastic chairs lined each of the two longer walls. I noticed a white square piece of cardboard with a large "z" on it fixed on the wall to our left as we entered. In front of the patient's chair was a new-appearing small piece of equipment on a tripod that immediately indicated a vision test.

The Doctor himself was a short, narrow little man of about fifty, with thin, sparse, graying hair, steel-rimmed glasses on his nose and a dour expression on his face. He wore a faded, checked, long-sleeved shirt open at the neck, with a stethoscope hanging around his neck. He did not rise when we walked in. He looked up and said *"Quieres?"* (What is it you want?). Melanie said *"Examen por favor."* The doctor glanced at each of us in turn, and back again, finally nodding his head at the chair beside his desk.

"You go first," I said to Toni, wanting to see what the procedure was before I sat down with this seedy individual. It was not that I was using her as a test lab, but being over eighty years of age I am very careful in such areas, knowing that the most innocuous question, wrongly answered, could negate my application.

I heard the usual litany of personal and medical questions, and realized that I had nothing to fear from this perfunctory "examination," and went outside to smoke my pipe. After about five minutes, I heard the "cacheck" of a stamp machine applied to paper, and entered again as Toni stood up and signed her form.

My turn. I sat down as the doctor took a new form from his small pile and ask my name. He spoke a modicum of English, and got irritated when I spelled out my name in Spanish. He repeated my letters in English, so I switched to English. He then repeated the letters in Spanish. He became confused and barked at me in rapid Spanish. I closed my mouth and waited. My name finally being written correctly, he filled out the rest of the address, telephone number etc. from my wife's form after ascertaining I was her husband.

He proceeded with "Do you drink?"

"A few times a week." I glanced over at the form as he checked the box *Consumo de alcohol*: "No."

"Do you smoke?" I answered, "I smoke a pipe", showing my prized Peterson. He checked the *Tabaco* box "No."

"Do you take medication?" I answered, "Only herbal medicines." He checked the *Medicamento* box "No."

At this point he asked me if I wore glasses to read and I replied "Yes." He then gestured at the tripod machine in front of me and I squinted leaning down to it, but could find no lens to look through. With some irritation he motioned to the wall at the end of the room fifteen feet away and I saw the 6" high letter "Z" bathed in light. I called out a loud "Z"!. He switched off the light and checked a box, then pointed to a row of three colored pins stuck in a cork on his desk and said "Color?" I called out the yellow, red and green pins in order. He said, with a certain smugness, that he only asks men about color because women do not have color blindness.

The doctor then rolled his chair close to me and applied the blood pressure cloth and pumped the valve. Satisfied, he jotted down numbers on the form, and then proceeded to mark the whole page of boxes with "X" and "0". He moved his stamp machine over the paper, slapped it smartly twice, and then pushed the paper to me to sign.

Melanie went through the same procedure, excepting the color question, of course. After she had signed the medical document I stood up and asked the price and the good doctor said 5,000 colones each. Melanie was politely indignant as she said "The man outside said 3,000." The doctor did not change his expression and said something in very rapid Spanish and repeated, 5,000 colones each. $10.00 for each exam. Exorbitant. We paid.

As we walked up the street complaining about the cost and laughing about the cursory exam, I counted the number of questions on the form that seemed to cover practically every part and function of the human body. There were 87 marks on the paper; most were "*No*", a few were "*Sí*" opposite untranslatable statements in Spanish. I read that I neither drink nor smoke, my blood pressure is 110 over 60, my pulse rate is 60 bpm (which he did not take), and that my vision is 20/20 (which he did not determine). Based on this examination I am one of the healthiest individuals in Costa Rica. We proceeded up the street and into the huge, dimly lit building.

Several long lines of patient people wound around the floor in different areas under the thirty foot high domed ceiling. High up on each side of the huge room a row of offices lined a balcony. Across the back of the room and down the side from the entrance were other rows of offices. One line of license applicants wound around a circular group of six computer stations in the center of the vast area. Each computer was attended by a neatly dressed young man, and piles of stacked paper. Asking a guard where new applicants go, Melanie instructed us to "That door where the guard is over there," pointing toward the far end of the huge room.

We walked over around the stations of computers, across the area to the rear of the room and entered a small office. Two people were at desks shuffling papers and talking. A very officious man wearing a tie (unusual except with bankers) told my wife to sit down, and motioned for me to go into his office behind the desks and wait. I entered and sat on the one chair and looked at the stacks of paper on his desk, on shelving, and on the floor. The white painted cement walls were bare of pictures of any kind. I saw a low stack of forms in English on his desk and took one to read. It was a recitation of the documents needed for a U.S. citizen applying for a driver's license. I saw that I needed my passport, U.S. driver's license, and a Residency Card, or, in lieu of these items, a certification notice that I had applied for Permanent Residency Status. I had this.

The official came in and quickly went over my medical examination form, then my passport, and then U.S. License, then asked for my Residents Card. I gave him my legal notice of application. The man said, *"No, no, Carta Residency, por favor."* I replied in my poor Spanish that I had not yet picked it up from my attorney, but (and I pointed at the certification of application) this is in place of the card. The man jumped up, thrusting my passport and papers at me saying *"No, no, no. Residency Carta es necessario,"* and he quickly ushered me out of the room. I grabbed the form in English saying that a certification of my residency application was sufficient – it was also taped to his wall – and pointed it out to him. "No, no, wrong, wrong," he said in English. "Wrong" as he pushed me out into the main area, my wife following.

"What happened?" she asked anxiously, fearing that I had angered a public official (which I had). I told her what happened, and that the guy said his own printed instructions were wrong. We agreed that the only thing to do was get our actual card and try again next week. So we walked back to Melanie in line and told her what had transpired. As we were talking she was called to sit in front of one of the young men and his computer station.

We walked to the wall and sat down in one of the dozens of blue, curved seat, bolted-together plastic chairs to wait. As I mentioned, Melanie was getting a five-year renewal of her CR license. She was seated at the station for 45 minutes as the young man laboriously worked on the computer after every question he asked of her. Every now and then she would turn and look at us, roll her eyes and shrug, tossing her head at the man seated behind the counter. We found out later he was a one-finger typist, and as a new trainee, was learning the whole process. After that long hour Mel finally stood up and smiled at us as she walked over to the Banco de Costa Rica station to pay the fee.

She pushed her completed forms under the glass at the teller window and asked what the fee was. A few minutes went by as the teller kept glancing at Melanie's forms then at his computer screen. Finally, he made a few terse comments and shoved the papers and money back to her and told her to go to a door marked Director of Administration, pointing out the location across the room.

She walked over to the wall of offices and knocked on that most imposing looking door. At this, a guard came running over and asked what she wanted. Then the door opened and a man peered at her with some irritation and asked what she wanted in rapid Spanish. They spoke back and forth, both Mel and Mr. Administration pointing at the bank teller's window. He kept shaking his head saying "No, no, no." Melanie turned and walked back to the bank teller. Again she presented her papers and cash. The teller took her papers and money, worked his computer, then again pushed them back through the window and loudly told her to go back to the administration door. Mel glanced at us and shrugged and again walked over and knocked, the guard hurrying back to protest her bothering the big man. Once again Mr. Administration came out and loudly told her to go to the bank teller for the processing, this time gesturing and scowling as he remonstrated with her for bothering him. He gestured and pointed. Mel told him the teller told her again to see him. The administrator pointed in the direction of the teller and loudly told her again it must be handled by the teller. Mel walked back a third time to the bank window, and started to give up her papers but the teller again said "No, no, no" and pointed once again to the Administration door.

Now Melanie had had enough. She walked halfway back to the administrator's office, stood in the middle of the floor and faced the computer stations. She shouted out loudly in Spanish "WHAT IS GOING ON HERE? WHERE SHOULD I GO?"

Two guards started running toward her, Mr. Director again flung open his door and stood with a scowl on his face, two of the computer attendants stood up and another one came from around his station and hurried to her. Mel again loudly shouted "WHAT … SHOULD…I…DO!" At this, the bank teller loudly proclaimed to the whole floor that she was not listed in the computer and so he could not renew her license that was not there, which was therefore not a license!

At this moment, down the hall and out of the door where we had gone to get our paperwork done, came the tie-wearing official who proved to be a Senior Supervisor. He hurried over to the loud voices and, joining in their volume and frustrated tone, asked what the problem was in very rapid Spanish. It was obvious that he was considerably irritated to have to deal with a "floor matter." Melanie tried to explain what she was told to do, and all the while the bank teller was loudly asserting to one and all that she did not have a valid license. The supervisor took Melanie's papers and scrutinized them carefully. He took her current license and examined it thoroughly. He asked Mel who had processed her paperwork. She pointed at the desk where she had sat for almost an hour but which was now empty. Then Melanie, the supervisor, the administrator, and two guards walked up to the bank window and the supervisor questioned the young teller about the problem. The bank teller pointed out that his computer showed no such number as a license.

The manager peered through the teller window and squinted at the computer screen that did not have her name or number. He again examined Mel's license. He pursed his lips and a deep frown came over his face as he thought for a full thirty seconds. Then, he led all five people around the circle of stations to the computer station where she originally had her paperwork done. There was no one there. It was nearing 4:00 o'clock, quitting time, and the young processor had apparently left for the day. The manager called out the name of the missing attendant loudly. There was no answer. Mr. Director of Administration shouted the name. Mr. Supervisor shouted out as well. Melanie joined in and shouted out the name they were calling, and finally one of the other attendants stood up and shouted as well. The building reverberated with shouts to which no one answered. There was an intense conversation by the supervisor and the administrator. They examined Mel's license. They walked back and again talked to the teller. Finally, the supervisor turned to the computer attendant at the next station and told him to redo the whole application. He walked Mel back to her original station and stood by as this new young man sat down and started asking her the questions on the form. I saw Mel point to the computer printout of her previous submission that had the answers, but the young man said "No, no" and pushed the forms aside, starting all over again with her name and address, etc. It would not do to compare the already printed form with her license to see if a word or number was possibly in error, then find the error and correct it in the computer, then print out the corrected application. The whole application must be again typed into the computer.

In the meantime, the hour was getting late. The other license hopefuls, still standing patiently in line as the time approached 4:00, were looking around anxiously, knowing that the closing time was almost upon them. At that point, Mr. Supervisor, having resolved Melanie's problem, turned to those in line and loudly called out that the camera (for their license picture) would only work for a few more pictures and then would be broken, and they must go and come back another time. Most of those that had waited in line for well over an hour, being Ticos, accepted the situation, and turned and walked to the door.

A neatly dressed young man, first in line with his wife who was holding a young baby, stood his ground and loudly complained that he had been standing there for more than an hour, that he had come from out of town, and he had a right to be processed. A guard hustled over at the angry voice and grabbed the young fellow by the arm and told him he had to leave. The young fellow resisted, and a shoving match began. The guard tried to pull the young man from his position at the head of the line, indicated by a black slash on the floor, but he was determined to keep his place. His wife also stood her ground behind him, the baby sleeping peacefully in her arms. The couple and baby were now alone, the other applicants had departed.

The pushing became more aggravated and the combatants took to calling out names at each other. The fray deteriorated to fisticuffs when the guard tried to yank the young man away. He threw a fist at the guard's shoulder, then they both flailed away with body blows; the guard's pistol flapping against his hip. Apparently having witnessed such altercations before, the idle computer attendants awaiting quitting time looked on with interest, but little excitement. Neither of the combatants did any damage. There seemed to be a rule that such fisticuffs are meant as a demonstration of one's indignation, and the guard took pains not to inflict so much as a bruise. It was, after all, only a citizen standing up for his rights against the bureaucracy.

Finally, after allowing a few minutes to exorcize the participant's frustration, the guard who had previously tried to protect Mr. Administrator for being disturbed, hustled over and the two of them immobilized the young man. This guard, having some seniority, told the young couple to go over and sit down in the row of chairs against the wall. They did, the angry young man calling out that he was going to stay there until he got his license.

Melanie's application, however, proceeded apace throughout all of this. She hardly glanced around at the disturbance; as a group, the employees watched the altercation between the guard and the young man with animated interest, talking among themselves about the situation. The supervisor stood by and watched the whole proceeding, keeping his eye on Melanie and her progress.

In half an hour, Mel's application was again completed (this processor could type with two fingers). She asked to see the printout herself, thoroughly checking the numbers, certification dates, etc. against her current license. It became obvious that the first processor had inverted two digits when putting the numbers of her driver's license into the computer. In that the application was incorrect, the supervisor had deemed that the whole application must be re-written, the wrong number could not simply be changed in the computer. Now, all information having been entered correctly, the small procession went back to the teller's window (that had remained open in case the matter was resolved). Melanie paid her fee, got everything stamped, got her picture taken (the camera having been resuscitated for this one flash), and received her license with smiles all around. Calls of *"Buenas tardes, buenas tardes"* rang through the building as the last of the employees ca-chaangd their time cards, and left. We did not look back to see if the obstinate young couple was still sitting by the wall. I expect they were.

On the return home we stopped by our attorney's office and found our Residency Cards had come in a few days ago. We signed the papers, were handed the cards, and shook hands with the attorney who said, "Now you are legally a resident!"

A few days shy of a month later we went back again to the motor vehicle building now armed with our Permanent Residency cards. We walked into the building crowded with long lines of patient Costa Ricans waiting for a license and went confidently over to the same office we had visited before. The same officious Supervisor glanced up from his desk as we walked in, then looked down at his work again. We sat down. Several minutes went by before a guard came up to us and asked what we were there for. My wife explained we were applying for a new license. The guard said, "You are in the wrong place. You must go to that office over there," and pointed to an open door at the far end of the building. Aha, a change in procedure.

We walked over to an open door and went into a short hallway with an office at the end. Another guard came over and asked us what we wanted. When we explained, he pointed out the office at the end of the hall. When we walked up to the closed door we heard the phone ringing. We sat down on the ubiquitous plastic chairs and waited. The phone kept ringing and I counted eight rings when a scowling, heavy woman walked up holding a cup in her hand. She juggled the keys and opened her office door, walked in and sat down in the chair. I was up to fifteen rings by this time, and watched her sip her drink, put it down on the desk, and casually pick up the phone. After a short conversation she hung up the phone, noticed us and motioned to enter and sit. She sorted through the several papers we presented, alternatively nodding and frowning. Finally she looked up at us and handed our papers back and said we needed to have copies made of our Permanent Residency cards. She told us to go out the building and up the street to the right to a commercial copy shop. We asked if copies could be made right there on the copy machine behind her desk, but were answered with "No, no, not possible." One assumes that the copy machines are not for the public. Too simple.

Toni asked "One copy of each on separate paper?"

"Oh no, put both copies on one piece of paper and I will cut it in half" she replied.

So out we went, up the street, into the copy store and got the required duplicates made. Back to the building again, across the room, down the hall to the office. We were again ushered in and handed all the papers over once again to the scowling woman who cut the copies in two, stamped each paper vigorously and told us now to stand in a certain line on the floor outside. We stood behind others, having faith the line would take us to the next step in the process. Our turn to be processed came and we walked over and sat down at one of the six computer desks in that circle in the center of the floor. A pleasant, smiling young woman took out papers and went through them. She smiled and handed the papers back to us and said they were not correct because we must have the reverse side of our Residency Permit copied as well as the front. We thanked her and said we knew where to get them copied, and we would be back. Out we went again, wondering why the woman in the first office didn't know to tell us we also needed copies of the reverse side. I suspect that it was not her department since she only needed to stamp the front side. Or, perhaps she was just "needling" these *Norte Americanos*.

We again went out and had copies made, came back and stood again at the end of the line, waited our way to the computer desk, got the work processed, then went to the bank line and waited again, paid our fee (everything being accurate), sat for the camera, signed the form, waited a few more minutes and were handed our plastic licenses. My picture was of a smiling Gringo. We had gotten Permanent Residency Cards – the *"Cedula"* – and Costa Rica Driver's Licenses! We were Ticos!

A road connecting villages

The Pan-American Highway

"This road is in bad shape" (above)
Another bump in the road (below)

A really bad road (above)
A roundabout (below)

A bad mountain road

A bridge

A roadside sign

Garbage and soil erosion

Soil erosion and deforestation

Construction

Assorted Events and Organizations

There is always some festival or other being celebrated in many towns and villages throughout the country – even each community will have its weekend commemorating its beginning, or revival, or something along with the national events and, of course, the numerous religious feast days. All of these are the most colorful, happy, lighthearted affairs with music, small parades, lots of indigenous food, arts, and booths of all kinds selling a myriad of items.

Of course the main weekends for holidays from work and parades and festivals are Easter Week and Christmas Week. "Nothing gets accomplished in December" we were told when inquiring about our visas. There is a splendid fiesta in Zapote on the east end of San Jose beginning December 25. The highlight is a bull fighting session in which about fifty men get into a makeshift bull ring and try to slap a bull with their hands, and sometimes with a nail-studded board. They set up a temporary hospital nearby, and have restricted the nearby bars and dance halls to only fifty! At Christmastime there is also an exceptional parade in San Jose. It goes on all day, featuring dozens and dozens of floats that would make New Orleans proud, and bands, dancers, life-size puppets, and more. One million people come from all over the country to San Jose each year to be part of this extraordinary festival. And Easter week is the same. The Catholic Church sponsors festivals and somber walks and processions throughout the land. Another major religious event for this Catholic country is August 2, when tribute is made to the Feast of the Virgin de Los Angeles – La Negrita, the black Madonna. Over the years two million people – that's half the population – trek to the city of Cartago about twenty miles east of San Jose to the basilica to pay homage.

For those organization-minded there are 59 clubs and organizations in CR – not counting six bridge clubs and umpteen AA groups. If you are an aspiring writer there are workshops for beginners and the advanced; there are screen writers workshops, and poetry workshops, book clubs, and so on. There are cooking classes and workshops of all kinds. As to other clubs and organizations, there are literally dozens! Every kind of organization from the frivolous (The Frisbee Club and The Hash House Harriers) to the serious (Truth Behind the News Discussion Club) and always the clubs for expats. For those fitness-minded, the exploding franchise "Curves" is cropping up all over the country. It is a "woman only" exercise operation. For all others there are "Gyms" in every town and city. "Spinning" (riding the stationary bike) is all the rage in CR at this time.

There are groups for studies in all religions, and there are churches of 23 different faiths throughout the Valley. All the happenings of the week are listed in the *Tico Times*. Throughout the year there are fine imported entertainments in theater, music, dance, film, and more. And, of course, practically every weekend there will be a fiesta somewhere in some village or other within an hour's ride for you. The Ticos love to be happy and love to celebrate it.

Time

This little matter is of such consequence here, I thought to take special note of it. We *Norte Americanos* have long been steeped in a rhythm of life that accounts for seconds. Since we were toddlers our slogans have been "Do it now." "Don't Waste Time." "Have a Strong Work Ethic." "Time is Money." "Efficiency!" and about 500 more. An ad for a drug that is currently running on U.S. TV has an objectionable guy running around saying "Too slow!" about different things, intimating that his antacid is really fast.

Earlier I wrote about the phrase our lawyer mentioned: living in leisure means more to a Tico than making money – the "work as little as possible" phrase. It seems shocking to you, I'm sure. North Americans have long been inculcated with the idea that to live is to work to be **successful**; that we are here on this Earth to make money and we had better get to work on it yesterday! Costa Rica is a culture that is exactly the opposite. I mentioned earlier that there are 17 holidays in CR throughout the work year – there are that many, not counting the weeks off for Christmas and Easter and the other fine national celebrations. Those days are for spending with the family, not for working, and it is rare that you will find a man who would rather earn more money, regardless of his financial situation, than be home with a day off.

Time is so very important here in its absentia, and it is so very important for newcomers to understand that when you plan to meet someone, and they set the time they will arrive, and they show up an hour later with smiles, happy to see you, but not one word about being late, well, you begin to understand what I mean.

It is not rudeness on their part, in fact it would be rude for you to mention their tardiness! This is a different culture. Get used to it. Relax. Enjoy life. There is one saying that means this culture, and Ticos use it as replacing "hello." It is *Pura Vida*. It means you are wishing a friend "the good life" (literally "pure life"). A lovely way to live. A relaxed, without stress way to live. A *tranquilo* way to live! It is also saying that a new *Norte Americano* must really adjust to a really different culture!

We have to remember that North Americans pride themselves that their operations are organized. They like everything in their lives to have structure and the element of time is critical to structure. In the hot climate zones, people are not structured, so they don't care if they plan a lunch for noon and the guests don't come until 12:30 or 1:00. And anyway, the host might not serve food until 1:30 or 2:00! Time is just not relevant to enjoying friends. This non-structured life means that life becomes a lot more spontaneous. And, from my personal observations of living in or traveling through a dozen or so countries, I do believe that these hot climate, non-structured, not organized people are happier. Really happier with themselves and with their lives.

I have a favorite true story about a friend in the U.S. who had a job offer from Hewlett Packard here (they have a large assembly plant in San Jose). She is in middle management and first complained about the salary offered being "only sixty some thousand dollars" (she was earning around $85K). After my telling her the standard of living in CR she calmed down and after a few more telephone talks and emails with HP she booked a flight a month away for the interview.

Later I emailed her and asked about what was happening and she replied "Well, I emailed [her contact at HP] that I would come down for an interview and gave him the date, and he didn't get back to me for a week! Then when I emailed him the time I would arrive, he took five days again to get back to me so I said to hell with it, if he doesn't care enough to reply to me promptly I don't need to work for that company."

I had to laugh and tell her that this was just standard in CR. If you had a month before your plane left there was no need for him to contact you immediately – maybe an American need, but not a CR requirement. We take things easy here. And, after all, if you talked to each other in a day or in two weeks, the plane would still take off on the day planned, so what was the big deal about the conversation? She just did not understand.

I also told her about a newly arrived neighbor who needed an attorney and I recommended ours at ARCR (see Supplement). Later I asked him how it turned out and he replied "I got another attorney. I had an appointment with yours, and I waited for 35 minutes and finally left. He didn't show up!" I thought I'd check with our attorney to get his side and he said "Yes, I had an appointment with your friend, but he was not there." I explained what had happened, but the attorney could not understand, saying "But I came to my office, why did he leave?" American culture up against *Pura Vida*.

A village street scene (but not typical)

Postal Services?

The post office is usually near the center of any town. Since there are no street names or house numbers there are no postmen and there are no corner mail boxes. There is very little mail. The main post office in San Jose, built in 1917, houses 15,000 P.O. boxes for this city of around two million people. It also has a fine stamp collection from around the world of one and one-half million stamps. In Heredia, a city of near 100,000 pop. the main post office has some 4000-5000 rental mail boxes. The cost to mail to the U.S. is around 45 cents. And it only takes a week or so to get the letter actually on a plane for the States. When you are mailing things, be aware that sending valuables or money is not really smart. It could be hazardous on either end when customs inspectors open your package to see if you are smuggling in …. whatever. It may never get to its destination. It has happened, and there is literally nothing you can do – there is no international mail insurance.

When you are receiving mail, things are also dicey here. Packages, even letters, can take anywhere from ten days to two months to get here (literally). And if it is something fine, there is a really good chance that you will never see it because of the local customs inspectors having first dibs. It is pretty common knowledge in this country that there is well-organized corruption in the Customs Department. Even getting a letter has it's hazards if the return address indicates anything concerning money. Letters I get from a financial planning corporation are opened regularly. The post office always places a tape across the flap reading *Recibido en mal estado* – "Received in a bad state." I know the flaps are always sealed with scotch tape so they will not come undone, so we know it was opened "for inspection." They are the only letters I receive that seem to arrive in a continual state of "bad repair." Postal people are just checking to see if any money is being transferred of which they should be aware. I would have my friend mail me some money and see if the letter ever gets through, but what would be the point?

The Customs Department must pay its employees very little. We know of an expatriate who opened up a business and after months of frustration in having the incoming shipments take months or never getting here, he went to the customs area and met with an inspector who set up an arrangement that whenever a shipment arrived he would call the expat and tell him what the "Duty" was. My friend was to then go to the bank and deposit the amount of the Duty in the inspector's personal bank account, telephone him that the money was deposited, and the goods would then be released. Very neat arrangement, and our friend paid about the same as the customs charge would be, but the inspector got the money instead of the government, and my friend got shipments promptly. It is a bad system and hurts the economy, and sooner or later some administration will be elected here that will see the economic sense of cleaning it up.

There are several postal systems available for getting mail from the States, all based in Miami, because the cost of a package mailed to and from Miami is about 40% less! Aerocasillas, UPS, FedEx, Jetbox, and Skynet, and maybe a few others. But you should ship big things like tables and sofas by sea – you will save around 50% off the regular air price. Many people here use one or the other of these services, especially if an expat has a business in the U.S. or here and gets packages or large envelopes all the time. Many people are satisfied, and many are not.

I have written a piece about my travails in getting a small package when I tried to use one of the big three "special delivery systems" here. This means that you pay small fee to a firm here and they establish a box in a Miami post office to which you direct all your U.S. mail. Then the company ships it here, routes it through customs, and has it delivered to your house. It's great in theory, and some say it works just fine. For me it was a disaster when I used the set-up that the ARCR has. The story about my experience follows this chapter.

Anytime traffic

Package Delivery Sir!

I may well be the only person in Costa Rica who smokes a pipe; only 15% of Ticos smoke cigarettes and not many smoke cigars. An expat from the U.S., I ran out of pipe tobacco, having smoked the last of a tin of tobacco a friend had sent from the States. After driving around to six shops in San Jose, Heredia, and points in-between where friends, acquaintances, and sympathetic neighbors said pipe tobacco might be found, I found a *farmacia* that had a 2 ounce pack of Dutch tobacco for $8.00. It lasted me five days.

So, I called a friend in the States and asked him to go to Walgreens Drug Store and buy me three of the 12 ounce Virginia Cavandish bags ($10.65 ea.) and send them poste haste via AeroCastilla, the private shipper that expedites a package through customs! Thirteen days after he mailed the tobacco to AeroCastilla's Miami address, we got the email notice that a package of tobacco had arrived! Huzzah! We made the hour run into San Jose and signed the papers at Association of Residents of Costa Rica (the ARCA mentioned earlier) to get it released from customs. They are friendly folks at ARCR, where members get a shipping discount. They receive packages, call and tell you it is there, and you run into San Jose, pay the bill and voila, you have a smoke!

The twelve mile trip from our home in the mountains usually takes 60-90 minutes each way, depending on the traffic. Four days went by before ARCR called again asking us to come back and sign a new form because the young man who was at the desk when we were there was only temporary and he gave us the wrong form to sign. We ruefully agreed to this as normal, so the next day back we went and signed the correct paper. Our apologetic clerk assured us things would progress promptly once we received the CR health certificate to bring in tobacco.

"No, no, no, no." I smiled, using Spanish iteration for emphasis. "We have been through that and it is not necessary!" I told him about having received tobacco some months ago and supposedly needing the health certificate. We ran down the proper health authority in San Jose who became exasperated at our request, pulled out a small post-it pad on which he wrote "No certificate needed" and soundly stamped it with the Health Institute seal. Having thoughtfully retained that official's card, I urged the ARCR clerk to call him. He did and the bewildered young man received admonishments over the phone and was told "Do not send those people over here!" This information was then telephoned in to AeroCasilla, and our trip to the Health Administration was obviated. We were assured the matter would now be expedited with all dispatch!

This being Costa Rica, it didn't quite work that way. Three days later we were told that there were "difficulties." The package was still in customs; there were wine glasses in the shipment as well, but the wine glasses were missing! After my saying there must be a mistake because we were not expecting wine glasses, we again drove down the mountain to ARCR and were handed invoices that indeed showed three packages of tobacco and four wine glasses from Cold Water Creek! Over the next two hours telephone calls were made to AeroCasilla about the confusion. The woman on the other end was adamant: three bags of tobacco and four wine glasses were on the invoice. HOWEVER, customs officials were very concerned that the package did not have any wine glasses in it! This immediately gives rise to *Theft*! Was the shipment tampered with at Miami? Was it inspected and rifled before it left the States? Could customs at the port of inspection in CR have purloined the wine glasses? This was indeed of great concern and no release could be made until the matter was completely resolved! We were told by the woman that she would pursue the matter and call us "in the next days" at our home. We drove back up the mountain talking about how maybe some wine glasses were sent as a belated Christmas present. But where were the glasses?

I telephoned my friend who was most apologetic after hearing about the situation. "I just used an old Cold Water Creek box to ship the tobacco in and guess I didn't take the old invoice out of the box for the wine glasses we bought. Sorry." I wanted to shout "Sorry doesn't help! This is Costa Rica man!" but, with great restraint, I thanked him for his effort and said it would all get straightened out.

Three days later we received a call from another very pleasant young woman who informed us she had resolved the whole matter. Of course, they have not yet found the wine glasses, so that was being investigated by customs. In addition, the package, with the wine glasses weighed over five kilos, so it was now considered something like (as far as I could understand her convoluted reasoning) a wholesale shipment of tobacco because of the weight, and was now being handled by "MAG" (an unknown acronym) whose warehouse was located two kilometers west of the cemetery in Heredia, then 200 meters north. I tried to explain in detail why there were no wine glasses, and that the three bags of tobacco weighed less than one kilo. It was in vain. There was an invoice for the wine glasses, so they must have been in the box and the weight was, as determined by Costa Rica Customs Department, over 5 kilos. About 12 pounds. (That weight was apparently on the invoice. With that much tobacco I could open a shop in San Jose).

Well, at least the smell of my Virginia Cavandish with 10% Kentucky Burley was getting stronger. The next day we got into our '86 Jeep and headed for the cemetery. Watching the mileage, we wound up in a small barrio, questioned a guard at a housing project about MAG who told us to go back to the light and turn east and in a few hundred meters we would see the building. We U-turned and headed back, turning at the one light, driving a while and finding … nothing. We were now in the countryside, peering at any and all buildings, large and small. Then we U-turned again and drove slowly back, figuring we might have maybe missed a very small MAG sign. Nothing. We saw a huge building perched back off the road with the word TRANSPORTAR emblazoned across the front. Well, transporters ship stuff, didn't they? So we pulled in and questioned the guard. "Of course MAG is here. This is Transportar." The guard proudly stated. We got a name tag and proceed into the building.

Inside the building we had some difficulty getting through to the several people behind the counter, albeit my wife's very good Spanish. A package sent by AeroCasilla caused confusion to this competing shipper. However, as luck would have it, several young women were coming down the steps on their way to lunch and one of them spoke English! We explained the situation and that our box was here. The young lady, all smiles, picked up the telephone and called someone somewhere. She brightly told us our box was indeed at Transportar, and in their warehouse, not in this warehouse, but in the warehouse by the airport in Alajucla. We were to go there and ask for Manuel, or Luis, as both spoke English. (We later found out that MAG was the Ministry of Agriculture).

Now we were on the scent. The field was narrowing. We hopped back in the car and proceeded to find the "other" Transportar. We were to drive past the Hampton Inn at the light, go through to the next light, then turn right and go down 100 meters. We did. There was no Transportars. Following the written directions exactly, we wound up on a small dirt road that led to a farmhouse. We turned around in the field and headed back to the light then went straight, guessing that the directions should have been turn left, not right, at the light. We were correct – an inviting Transportar was just ahead.

Inside the building, asking for Manuel, we sat and watched the busy scurrying of well-dressed young people busily transporting. Finally a young man, all smiles, walked up to us, hand extended, said he was Luis, and listened to our story. He carefully examined the invoice papers we presented. "Well," he said, "Yes, your package is here. We have it." He examined the documents again and said, "Wait here one moment" and disappeared. Five minutes went by before he strode back, all smiles with forms in his hand. "Please, sir, just sign this form and we will send the papers to customs and get your package released." I signed, and he said "I will call you tomorrow."

Tomorrow came and went, but the second day I got a call from Manuel. He asked after my health, my family, and my state of mind, then said "*Senor*, we need the invoice showing how much you paid for the tobacco." I paused, mentally working out how I would explain the situation. "Manuel," I said, "the tobacco was purchased in the U.S. for cash. There are no receipts, maybe just a machine slip for the transaction."

I had given him an opening upon which he seized "Exactly, Sir! We need that receipt. Please obtain it and then bring it to us and we will immediately release your package."

I again said that the tobacco was purchased in the States, and he replied, "I should not say this, sir, but many things can be done with a computer, if you understand ....?" I said I would try and get a receipt for him. "Excellent, excellent!" We hung up.

That evening I found the Walgreen site on the internet, downloaded a page showing their "Walgreen" logo, pasted it over and made up a cash slip in minute type, and voila, we had a cash receipt including a sales tax in red – a real (almost) Walgreens sales slip! The next day we drove down to Transportar and met Manuel (by this time he and Luis were interchangeable). He examined the slip carefully, beaming all the while as we explained that we had found the receipt which had been received in the mail some days ago. Manuel carefully clipped the small receipt to the now burgeoning stack of papers and invoices, and said he would immediately forward this to customs and our package would be released.

Only two days later we received a call from Luis who said we needed to come down and sign a form for the release of the package. I thought a moment, but decided any protest would be futile, so told him we would be there the next day at 10:00 am, and thank-you-very-much.

We were prompt. This time it was indeed Luis who smiled his way through asking about the states of our health and the pleasant day. He then presented me with a blank sheet of paper, "Just sign anywhere ... here," his finger pointed to the middle of the page. "But this is a blank paper," I said. "Of course, yes, it is. This is necessary for your release," he smilingly replied. Now, having been in Costa Rica for a few years I am no longer surprised at anything required in this very convoluted, twisted, maze of bureaucratic tangle in which the government and business operates. Anywhere else signing a blank piece of paper would be tantamount to giving away your house. But here, it can be considered business as usual. I signed because it was probably a check of my signature with the one I had signed at ARCR for the initial release – which he held in his hand – among all the papers. Luis said goodbye with smiling assurances that he would call within a few days and tell us to come pick up the package.

Four days went by before the telephone call came. My friend on the other end of the phone was now Manuel wishing me well and asking after my family. I asked him how the process was coming along. He immediately got down to business and assured me my goods were released from customs, although they had not yet found the wine glasses. I could come and collect the package with payment of the customs, tax, the three weeks storage fee, postage, handling by AeroCasilla, handling by Transportar, charges for inspection, transportation, the telephone calls, and a few other minor costs. He said "You will have to bring the money and it will be sent to customs before we can release your package. I am sorry, but we have to have your cash first to be sent to customs."

I sighed, thinking of driving down again to give the money, and then yet another trip to pick up the package. I think the total trips would be around a dozen to receive a package in the mail. Routine. "Okay, how much are the charges?" Manuel paused, and answered in a strong, authoritative baritone, "Two hundred fifty dollars American".

I said "How much did you say?" It didn't change: $250.00 for a package of three bags of tobacco that cost around $30 in the

States!

I won't relate the next minutes of my explaining the retail value of the tobacco; that we had previously had a shipment of 16 ounces of a can of tobacco with a customs charge of $10.00; about the exorbitant customs fee of $150 (!); or about his handling fee of $50.00. In the end, frustrated, seeing my evenings of filling my custom-made-limited-edition-Peterson-gem-of-a-pipe go up in smoke, I shook my head at the telephone and said, "Manuel, keep the tobacco. I will not accept it. This is an outrageous charge. I'm sorry, *buenos tardes*." I hung up.

Perhaps in the shade of one of the buildings at Transportar a warehouseman is enjoying his first pipe of tobacco. Perhaps somewhere in the customs labyrinth, clerks are being questioned about their wine-drinking habits.

I am adapting to dried palm leaves.

The Water Department!

One of the things that brought us here was that the travel books said that the water was potable throughout Costa Rica. That may have been the case years ago, but is not so any more. **At least 40% of the water in this country is not potable**. The government has never specified where this non-potable water is. And the government admits that **97% of the "black water"** – waste water mixed with toilet, hospital, and other sewage – **flows directly into the rivers and streams** throughout Costa Rica without treatment. Even with this known fact an official recently said "Our main concern is the hydrocarbons and chemicals and industrial contaminants;" there is no testing for this, even in San Jose, although the city gets water from the outlying agricultural areas. So we buy bottled water now – at the beach or in our home area! We have friends who live on the edge of a small village at about 4000 feet who recently had a private company test their water and found it was contaminated with e-coli and toxins. They ordered a Reverse Osmosis system from the States.

I write about the water problems at the beaches in a later chapter, but the potable water problem can be country-wide. In most rural areas there is no such thing as a water department. We live outside a lovely little village on the slopes of a volcano and get our water from a large tank that comes from a gushing spring a few kilometers up the mountain near the top of the volcano, and it is presumably pure – at this time. There is a small group of people, some Ticos, some Gringos, who informally meet every so often and talk about how the water is, that the pressure seemed down a bit last week, etc. They have no means to test the water for purity, they have no repairman that can be sent to address a broken water line (which is a plastic tube about ¾" in diameter that runs along the side of the road) – when there's a problem, someone always calls the someone (I have yet to find out who) in the large city ten miles down the mountain who gets up here in a day or so.

The local water committee does not know what the water table level is, the storage capacity in the tank up the hill, if the supply will last, what the water pressure is, what the gpm rate is, or anything else technical. But they are a water committee and that is a start to getting a handle on possible problems in the future.

We trust that what everyone says is correct: the water where we live is pure. We haven't, so far, had ill effects from drinking it. But someday in the future, and my guess is the near future – because all the waste water, grey and black, gets poured either into the ditches along side the road or into a nearby stream or river – there will be an official acknowledgment that **all** water in Costa Rica could be contaminated. The government is probably not sure where the pollution is, and 97% of ALL the sewage throughout the country flows into ditches and sewer lines that run directly into streams and rivers that flow eventually into the ocean. The hospitals have no better system to deal with their seventeen tons a day of sewage – four tons of biological waste per day in San Jose – which can mean much more serious contamination. The local paper carried an article about the problem and noted that "34 counties, from San Jose to the smallest town, dump their sewage into the Rio Grande De Tarcoles." It flows to the ocean. A central disposal system for San Jose was to have been built in 2005, but nothing yet. And it appears that the trash dumps in other cities fare not much better. Forty-five percent (that's almost half!) of the population does not have sewers. A government official was recently quoted as saying "The vultures in Costa Rica provide an important service in disposing of dead animals and garbage." Now there's a disposal system to rival Waste Management, Inc.!

The aquifers in the Central Valley are being depleted. One government study estimated that in only eight years the consumption will more than equal the aquifer's replenishing by 15%! (That's based on **today's usage**, and not taking into account the construction now under way, and planned, that will draw from those aquifers). Plans are being made to develop studies to determine possible measures that might have a positive effect on water use. The perfect bureaucratic answer.

Then there is what the government considers a larger problem in contamination – that by industrial contaminants, hydrocarbons, and chemicals. In 2004 there was a gas station storage tank leak affecting 320,000 people that still has not been resolved. There is just one (1) employee to monitor 336 gas stations in CR. But the problem of hydrocarbons (which are naturally occurring compounds found in solvents, waxes, and oils) are looming larger in that they cannot be detected by smell or color. The country has to call in outside experts from the U.S. – the EPA! Could this be the blind leading the blind?

There was a large explosion and fire at a chemical plant in the Central Valley a month ago that officials are still "investigating" – there has been no environmental assessment, and no clean-up process has started. The government disorganization and red tape and the lack of communication between agencies has plagued CR's handling of chemical related disasters for years, according to Federico Paredes, the president of the Costa Rica Association of Public Health (a private agency). To date the government does not know what chemicals were involved, much less have a handle on how to clean them up – that is the function of the Health Ministry. The *Tico Times*, however, did get a partial list. The hundreds of thousands of gallons of water that were poured on the fire mixed with the chemicals and flowed into the rivers, which flow into the ocean. It happened over a holiday so no one took samples to find out how polluted the river was – and then it rained the next day. A statement to ease fears was put out by Mario Leiva, president of Environmental Tribunal: "… it can take years before the contamination reaches the aquifers. In the meantime, tests are technical and expensive." Now that's a CR approach!

The water tables throughout the country lie mainly under the major rivers. Most of the potable water comes from these water tables. Some enterprising entrepreneur will soon make a fortune selling RO (reverse osmosis) units to the few hundred thousand people who can afford them. And then, after the pollution shows e-coli, bacteria, pesticides and other toxins, perhaps then, the government will start to plan on construction of water purification plants, and will begin building sewage treatment plants throughout the land. Then they will start regulating the chemical industries and the many other factories that use chemicals in their manufacturing process and pump it out to the sea. As always, not until there is a severe problem will this situation be addressed. Many of the newer homes like ours have their own septic systems, the effluent going into the ground which will, sooner or later, get into the ground water. Ah, the benefits of living in a "developing" country!

When eating out, my suggestion is to order bottled water at the table. Of course, the newer large and modern hotels and resorts will loudly/proudly proclaim they will have their own "sewage treatment operations" – ground septic systems (and back-up generators for the electric outages). But can you believe them? Even so, very, very few of the small and older hotels have any adequate disposal of their waste and sewage water, not to mention in-house water purification systems.

Exactly where the contamination is – in or near what communities – is not known. There are several water testing laboratories listed in the telephone book, and a few companies that sell water purification systems. One official recently said the government would soon have to have regular testing done on some government facilities.

I do know that the beach communities where there are larger populations with resorts and hotels, etc. have a real problem **now** according to those who live there (see "Life's a Beach"). Elsewhere I mentioned our water being rationed at our Tamarindo hotel last year. We do not drink tap water in any low lying community, and I take quick showers when in a hotel. Most people don't know it, but the skin can absorb seven times the contaminants in a shower as one will ingest from drinking an eight ounce glass of water. Since we visit the beaches or dine out infrequently we have not started to worry … yet.

Downtown Heredia

Doctor, Doctor!!

This is a big reason for many to move here. The government health care system is certainly adequate and very inexpensive! When we arrived my wife and I took the CAJA insurance – the government health insurance costing $18.00 a month, and everything was covered. I used it a few times for congestion brought on by my moving from twenty years of desert climate to one where the humidity is always around 90 %. But for something serious, such as having an operation, you get in line. If it is not life threatening, you will wait a month or two or three. If you need immediate care you will be taken immediately (and then you will wonder whether the government doctors are as good as the private hospital doctors). In a recent article in the paper a health official talked about the need to bring the government hospitals up to the level of those in the U.S. and he said that if the money was available it would take **about 11 years**. And the U.S. health system was recently evaluated at #37 in the world – just ahead of Costa Rica!

We do use private hospitals and doctors now when needed – as do virtually all the expatriates – and all the Ticos we know. When I had a melanoma cancer on my forehead – found by a private dermatologist's check-up – the whole bill for the 1hr:15 min. procedure for the surgeon, anesthesiologist, nurse, and use of the OR – was $250.00 in a fine private hospital. I was hooked up to every kind of monitor known to man.

But to spend a night in the CIMA or Biblica Hospitals (two of the best here) it will cost $200-300 for a private room including the charges for everything from a Kleenex to the food you eat, just like anywhere, and for a two night stay, a doctor spending some time with you, and all the tests that Western medicine needs, it can run around $1,000.

We have even been to a Medicine Man, locally known as "the witch doctor" – he studies you carefully, and if you are a female he checks your breasts out with great care for possible lumps! When he finishes his exam he gives a message that would break bones anywhere else, and then rubs what smells like Absorbine Jr. on the area. I was taken back to my high school locker room. "The Witch Doctor" piece follows this chapter.

A revealing method used by all the doctors here, wherever trained and whatever specialty, is that they will take an hour with you and ask a lot of questions that have nothing to do with an illness, but are about who you really are, do you go to church, how do you feel about living here, where do you live, what do you eat, are you happy, do you travel, how's your sex life, and on and on. I got irritated at first because of – compared to U.S. doctors – the personal intrusion. Then I realized that MD's here know that there are many factors affecting health aside from the obvious – such as that you have laryngitis. They try and figure out why you got laryngitis! Wow, what a concept, I thought. A doctor who really seems interested in what made you sick! Fantastic.

People are always asking us about "dengue," the mosquito-born disease that can kill you. Up here on the mountain we don't have mosquitoes, but they are a real bother at the seaside and in the low-lying areas and coastal regions. In the first 4 ½ months of this year almost 8,000 cases of the fever have been reported – up 115% over last year. It probably will not get any better because of the early and heavy rains so far this year. In fact, one heralded annual festival was cancelled recently because of the dengue outbreak. The head of the Public Health Ministry recently said that it was the most important thing for people to clean up the areas around their homes and communities; that preventing dengue is "as much a citizen's job as it is the ministry's." So there you have the government approach.

The country is known for the quality of its plastic surgery and dentistry. We know of several people who have flown in and had extensive dentistry and/or cosmetic surgery done because the quality of the surgery was so good and the price was so inexpensive that they had money left over after all the costs of getting here.

There are health insurance companies and the cost is about one-quarter to one-third what it would be with a stateside HMO. The private hospitals are exceptional, have the most modern equipment, and doctors trained in CR, U.S., and Europe. But mainly, everyone associated with a hospital stay, everyone, is genuinely warm, helpful, interested, and caring! From doctors to receptionists, nurses, et al, people act like they are really concerned that you may have a problem.

Costa Ricans will spend around $475 Million in 2007 on private health care. This is a telling statistic about the government health care system. Ticos spent a lot of that figure on medicine (the U.S. drug companies advertising campaigns have reached this tiny country), followed by dentistry.

You should be aware of alternative medicine here. It is a large part of the treatment in CR for anyone who cannot afford more than the CAJA $18.00 a month. And, the anomaly is that the government does not recognize that there are hundreds, maybe thousands of alternative doctors doing Acupuncture, Homeopathy, Holistic Medicine, Naturopathy, and other more esoteric natural medicine treatments. Some alternative medicine doctors have practiced in CR for decades and have exceptional followings, but are not listed anywhere. There are no lists of doctors and practioners of any of these treatments; there is no advertising, no name in the phone book, no signs in the window of the house or building where they practice. Many have studied in and have degrees from the U.S. and Europe and are the best you can find anywhere in the world.

There is a story going around about why acupuncture is not recognized. It seems that a decade or so ago an acupuncturist located in one of the major suburbs of San Jose became very successful. The local M.D.'s, seeing their practice (and income) decline, prevailed upon friends in government to declare acupuncture the equivalent of *persona non grata*. The acupuncturist had to relocate somewhere else. And so, ever since, this 3000 year old proven medical treatment has had to work in the shadows.

The obvious result of the government not dealing with this form of medicine is that they are losing all the sales taxes and income taxes by these probably thousand businesses. These doctors have to have their supplies, such as acupuncture needles, smuggled in from other countries. If you want "alternative," just start asking your new expat friends where you can find any kind of treatment you want. Most in our circle of friends use alternative medicine after they try it.

The dentist profession must be crowded. As one North American told me when we came here, "There are as many dentists as there are Chinese Restaurants, and they're on every corner." (The presumption is that all the Chinese who were brought in to build the banana company railroads stayed here and opened restaurants). True, there are a lot of dentists. The dentistry is supposed to be very good, from cosmetic surgery to implants, from getting a filling to dentures. They are quick and inexpensive and the work – at least my work – has been exemplary. Ask around for the name of a good dentist and you will find as many "… I swear by …" as you will talk to.

A street vendor

The Witch Doctor

He is a wizened, thin, little brown man not five feet tall wearing neatly pressed brown trousers and a faded blue shirt, buttoned to the top and at the wrists. Sparse white hair covers his head, and he wears thick leather sandals on his brown bare feet. He is a Medicine Man to the indigenous population scattered on the fringes of the Central Valley. He is known to the North American expatriate community as the "The Witch Doctor," and many of the expatriates have, at one time or another, gone to him for a variety of ailments.

Be assured, he is a genuine "natural healer" who learned from his father who learned from his father, and so on back through generations of native healers. He speaks no English, and says little in a different dialectic of Spanish. He mainly looks at his patient, then touches him where he has already detected (by some divination) there is a problem. He uses a type of acupressure to determine where he will push, knead, and mold. Sometimes he starts working well away from where you think he should be, and believe me, that little man has the strength of a small ox.

He lives in a very modest home along with a group of houses on the outskirts of Alajucla, the third largest city in Costa Rica. His home neatly kept; the grass and shrubbery trimmed, wicker chairs on the patio for his clientele. As is typical in this country, no sign announces the profession of the occupant practicing alternative medicine.

The gate is open, which is unusual because every house in CR is ringed with an iron fence and an imposing gate that is kept locked. You walk up the short walk to the patio and call out, then sit down in the shade and wait. Soon "the doctor" opens a door with no outside doorknob, and looks at his potential patients who give a smiling *Buenas dias*. He replies in the same and somehow knows which one is the patient and beckons that person into his office.

The office is a small room with a linoleum floor, a large poster of male musculature on one wall, a bare wood chair in a corner next to a small table, and a cracked leather-covered table with a faded floral design pillow against the other wall. He motioned for me to take off my shirt and lie face down upon the table. What proceeded over the next twenty minutes would convince anyone that this man knows what he is doing!

I had heard of him a year ago at one of the ubiquitous luncheons that U.S. and Canadian expats give. Acquaintances told us about someone having recently gone to "this odd little man," a "real witch doctor," and "he absolutely fixed my sprain so that in a few days I was actually walking normally ... etc." Such commendations were not to be taken lightly! A few weeks later a friend said she was going to the Witch Doctor to see about her knee, which had been bothering here for years, and would we like to come along. We would!

We sat quietly in the small patio, and when our friend came out she said she had a real relief and turned to pay the 3.000 colones (about $6.00). The "doctor" shook his head and motioned me into his office. I laughed and said "Oh, no, doctor, there's nothing wrong with me." Of course, he does not understand a word of English and just kept motioning me in, so I went. For six dollars I would take a treatment whether I needed it or not!

To make the story short, after fifteen minutes of pushing

and pulling my shoulders and arm, twisting and messaging (more like Rolfing) my neck and shoulders with something that smelled exactly like Absorbine Jr., he stood back and motioned for me to turn my head to the right.

I should tell you that for about forty years I have not been able to turn my head more than 45 degrees to the right because, as the x-rays show, I have a fusion of two vertebra in my neck. Somehow, when I was a child I fell, or had one of my many accidents, and caused the problem. I have long lived with half turning in my seat to look to the right when driving when I need to see what is coming.

So I smiled at him and turned my head 90 degrees to the right … with no pain! I turned it front, then back again 90 degrees! Then I turned it 90 degrees to the left, figuring that somehow he took the ability to turn from my left side and gave it to the right, because it was not possible that I could turn my head like that. Every doctor since I was a kid said I couldn't even have surgery for it. And I had no pain. None! And I could even snap my head to the right! He was a witch doctor, for sure! I hurried out of his office and showed Toni what the man did. He just stood there and smiled a little enigmatically. For the first time in living memory I could turn my head all the way to the right with no pain!

Well, there you have our medical anomaly. He was good for me and for others. There are, however, some who raise their eyebrows when we mention the little man. And I must admit my second adventure with him was not as productive. I recently had a fall and tore some shoulder muscles and tendons, and decided to see what the witch doctor could do for it. Wrong choice. It seems that his style of medicine has one way of treatment for everything – heavy message, strong pushing and pulling. He gave a sharp yank on the sore arm and shoulder and damn near put me on the floor in pain! The shoulder obviously didn't get better after that "treatment" so I went to a sports medicine M.D., had an MRI and found that I indeed had torn some muscles and the rotator cuff. Yanking on it was not a beneficial move.

So now when someone says they heard I know a really good doctor who is a Medicine Man, I smile and suggest that there may be certain limitations to his treatments.

Expat's Social Life

We moved here from a quiet social life in the States. Within three weeks of our arrival one of the expatriates telephoned and invited us to a luncheon. It was our introduction to a social custom that has been going on for years and is the basic and staple of the social life for most Americans here – "The Luncheon."

About 25 – 30 people gather at someone's home around 12:30 p.m. Immediately drinks of his or her beverage of choice are served and the social chatter starts. It comes so easily because everyone knows everyone in the room. About 70% of the party people are wine drinkers, and 70% of them are white wine drinkers – the average being 1 ½ bottles per guest! The luncheon is served around 2:00 - 2:30 p.m., usually as a buffet, and the food will be excellent. The people sit in groups, most of them totally relaxed and easy and conversational, and subjects will usually start with a short dose of U.S. politics; then it flows about everything from places to eat to auto mechanics. After coffee and dessert the after-dinner drinks come out, usually in profusion. Hard to turn down a "Have you tried this brand of cognac?" when you see that it's a 70 year old treasure. And then more conversation, which by this time will turn to "Where are we going this year?" – in that people here travel a lot. A LOT. When you hear some one say "Well, not Paris this year," and another chimes in "Nor China please," and a third, "Not Argentina ... let's think Africa," you know this crowd has been around. My wife and I just smile and murmur "Yes, that would be nice to do next summer." As I have indicated, most of the expats we know or have met, perhaps a hundred or so couples, are retired, fairly affluent, and vary in age from the middle 60's to 80.

We will never forget that first luncheon because both of us, being new, meeting all new people and wanting to fit in, just kept smiling and saying thank you every time someone filled our wine glasses. We got absolutely snockered and managed a stable – sort of – withdrawal at 5:00 p.m. when most took their leave (who were also pretty much in the tank). I made a very careful negotiation of the short drive from the party place to our new home. We promptly went to bed and slept the night through.

That was the beginning of a round of luncheons over the year, and after the first flurry of invitations – we were on the "A" List there for a while – we sort of settled into what we call the "B" List and averaged a luncheon a month. (The "A" List gets 2 - 3 invites a month and 2 - 3 a week at Christmas time).

As in most groups, there is always a leader or two, and in the social scene on this side of the Central Valley it is "the Grande Dame Diana." A widow in her late 70's, wealthy, attractive, and "to the manor born." One does not drink beer from a bottle at Diana's palatial estate, and many even wear a jacket to her afternoon soirees. (I have worn a tie twice in a year and a jacket once!). When the invite came – if it did – for an overnight stay at one of her rare evening parties, you had "made it." You were set for party invites from the others. And I am pleased to say that in due course we were indeed invited for an overnight! A gentile evening of good conversation, a luxurious bed for a night's sleep, and lovely breakfast in the morning before we made our goodbyes. We really do care for that kind lady.

The mix of expats is really interesting. There are retired

oil men, psychologists, actors, government employees, widows of wealthy entrepreneurs, real estate magnets, men who built businesses into chains and then sold, airline pilots, artists, even retired rare book gallery people who have turned writers! One of the other special people in our group of twenty or so is the widow Dolly who lives on a fine estate and annually gives a benefit, having about 125 people over, who pay $75 for the pleasure. It is always a treat for us to be invited during the year to one of her lunches of 30 or so people.

At first I wondered what in the world everyone found to talk about after the third or fourth affair, but I soon found out that interesting conversation flowed fairly smoothly, the vocal machinery always being oiled with a single malt or "Stoli's," then a bottle of Chilean Chardonnay, and it all topped off with a brandy snifter half full of Bailey's Irish Cream or that Napoleon brandy after dinner! The food is always excellent and plentiful, and we never want supper later. After the second year we now sip soda and lemon until the food is served, then a glass or two of wine, and that is it. We have a much more enjoyable time listening to conversations that flow from investments (always comes up in a certain group of men), to trying to grow orchids, to recipes. And after three years we are very fond of most of our crowd. We are only getting invites every few months, and that is fine. We enjoy our several more personal friends only two or four at a time for dinner, and more and more we most enjoy being by ourselves. It is the good life here. As Ticos say, *Pura Vida.* Should you come to live here, look us up and we'll have a luncheon for you!

Aside from the afternoons described above, using the computer, watching TV and reading is about all folks here do when they are not traveling – very few have a social club they belong to, or sports clubs such as golf or tennis. Relaxed living is a way of life for most of the expatriates. You can only get the local Cabletico (TV) monopoly that supplies all local stations and cable to subscribers. They have a menu that touts itself as "impeccable programming," which means that you don't know what will be on TV that night. They have advertised programs for six months that never appeared. They announce movies on Cinemax and HBO that never show and they run something else. There is the standard programming that we have gotten used to, but every now and then they simply start showing something else, without explanation. And the ESPN2 with a Latin flavor seems to be absolutely nothing but commercials – for ESPN2! Constant self-promoting commercials. Of course they do show soccer (*futbol*) games from around the world a lot of the time (and advertise ad nauseam ahead of every game!), but we do get to watch U.S. baseball, basketball, tennis, boxing, figure skating, and more. You will get CBS and ABC network stations and HBO, lots of movies and CNN and C-Span. Pretty good TV, all things considered. I will say that cable does cut out – go black – a few times in a month – there are a lot of electric problems in this country. And I expect it will get worse before it gets better as the country is expanding so rapidly and as more and more hotels, high rises and mansions get built to accommodate the influx of North Americans. And if you should buy or rent where RACSA "has no service" there is always the dish for satellite viewing. You won't get CNN but you will have tons of movies.

We all live with the computer – even those in their 80's here are computer literate to a degree. People email each other around the country and to friends and relatives in the States. We found an excellent, top drawer, really high quality computer technician so that when anything goes wrong it gets fixed right! He's Tico, speaks excellent English, really knows his business, and has reasonable charges. We couldn't have gotten along without him. Of course, he was referred to us from another *Norte Americano*. We have had him and his wife over for dinner, and had our housekeeper and her husband over for afternoon coffee before we both decided she would like to work for us – her husband is a U.S. expatriate – not an unusual thing here since people are more casual, although the wealthy Ticos have a severe class line. I noted elsewhere in this book that Ticos are of all colors, from the blondest blonde to the blackest black skin color and a hundred shades in between. One never ever thinks about, or even notices skin color here. It is a nice way to live among friends.

Construction of Oceania Condominiums

Cost of Living

When we came here all those years ago the travel books said one could live comfortably on $900 a month! Given that the books were two years old I figured $1,000 or so would be an accurate figure. Four years later it is "higher and risin," no matter what the travel books tell you. To give you a quick idea about the **real** costs, I have listed our averaged out monthly bills:

Gas	$75.00
Electric	30.00
Water	5.00
Trash Collection	-0-
Telephone/Internet	35.00
Cable	30.00
Cell Phone	10.00
Food	375.00
Rent	650.00
Car Gas	80.00
Medical	100.00
Car Repair	150.00
Entertainment	150.00
Miscellaneous	200.00
Housekeeper/Gardner	150.00
Total monthly living cost	$1,985.00

You might look at this list and think you won't have the car repair cost because you have a relatively new car – wrong! The roads destroy the computers, shocks, springs, tires, and everything else that is even mildly sensitive in a car. You might also think you will not have the medical cost. If you take out the private health insurance that is available, it will cost on average $175 a month for a 60 year old. True, you might not need it, but it is a fact that many of us immigrants get lung congestion that lasts for a year or more because of the high humidity; they get digestive problems with the different type of food; and sometimes this relaxed living with "really nothing to do" gets to people and they wind up needing a sedative, of all things. Or the frustrations here lead to a sedative!

We consider ourselves lucky to have a lovely 2500 sq. ft home, landscaping, and great view, and have this low a living cost. As I have written elsewhere, one can find any life style one desires in this country. Some of our friends have million dollar mansions, most are in the 500K range, and a few are in the 250K range. Our home value is in the lower figure. Keep in mind that a half-million dollar house in Costa Rica is something very grand indeed! In a recent article in the *Tico Times* an expat was building a house and ran into problems of all kinds, including break-ins of his half constructed home when he was in the States (ALWAYS have someone stay in your house when you are not there!). He remarked that house building, with all the problems, was cheaper here, but everything else was expensive.

The first three years we were here the *colon* – the local currency – devalued about one-third – 10% a year. Then, the new president Arias de-regulated it and let the currency float free and it has held steady, although it is now following the dollar in devaluing. Inflation still continues at about 10% a year and it does not seem that the government is doing anything really effective to corral it.

And then there are the usual "It can't have happened" things that go wrong with regularity for which there is no budgeting. We go to the ATM to withdraw $400 in American dollars. We press all the right buttons, but it gives us only $250.00 although the receipt shows $400. We go into the bank and show it to the manager (who knows us by this time) and he says "Not to worry [I love these people!] even though you put in that you wanted $400 your balance will only show the $250 you got." (They will only tell you something that will please you!) Of course, at the end of the month the damned machine recorded a withdrawal of $400! Now the trick is to try and get it straightened out, which cannot be done because banks only look at slips of paper, and the **customer is never right here** (at all stores, institutions, banks, etc.). The bank manager here will not remember anything.

That statement about the customer not being right is true. We have found the only one store that will take anything back and that is PriceMart, owned by Costco. If you buy something at all stores in Costa Rica and you don't like the way it works, or if it doesn't work, there is no taking it back and getting a refund. You can get another of the same, but never a refund, no matter if it was delivered and the delivery man dropped the appliance off the porch. He will tell you to take it up with the owner, but the owner lives at the beach. Somewhere.

A truck and bus accident

Notes in Passing

Many, if not most, **gas stations** in CR are just that – gas stations, and they don't even change a tire. Some Shell stations have convenience stores with them – obviously for tourists because the prices are high.

Linens, and cloth for curtains, etc. are sold in specialty stores such as Yamuni in San Jose, but they don't sell needle and thread to make the curtains. It is assumed that if you have the money to shop at Yamuni you will hire someone to make the curtains and that person will never shop at Yamuni, thus no needle and thread. Logic. Such items are purchased at a local *pulperia* – the has-everything tiny local grocery

There are dozens of **hardware stores** everywhere – *ferreterias* (*ferre* from the Latin for iron) but not one will have what you want. Most in the small towns and cities are small and only stock things in local demand, and I have no idea what they are. But there are huge ones here and there, so ask around.

You will see "**Dry Cleaning USA!**" in the larger towns and cities. The prices are high, but that's because *Norte Americanos* and the rich Ticos use it.

For almost anything American in a **grocery store** go to AutoMercado – I mentioned this in the food section – higher cost, to be sure – a box of Honey Bunches of Oats cereal will cost around $7.00, and they have an excellent liquor section and feature wines from Chile although you can find a Napa or Sonoma sometimes, and sometimes even French of a lesser quality. Also, you will enjoy the free samples. It is the custom here for the supermarkets to have young ladies walking around with trays of lunch meats, cereals, cookies, fried meats, desserts, and even a thimble full of a liquor – on Fridays and the weekends. I do enjoy the snacking – it relieves the real crush of people that are always shopping those days (walk around a large store twice and you have gotten dinner!).

You will **need a car** if you do much running around at all. Talk to friends, check the papers for someone moving out of the country and leaving his car, and then have the car checked over twice.

If you decide to **buy property** then get an expatriate-recommended lawyer and question everything. Land titles in this country are often very convoluted and tied up from generations of selling and re-selling when there was little surveying, and inaccurate boundary markings, not to mention the scams and crooked dealings. Of the one million lawsuits pending in the courts, many are said to be land disputes, so be sure of a clear title!

When you decide to **take a trip** and see some of the sights, talk to expats here about where to go and where to stay – very important – and what the prices are. Then call ahead and make a reservation and **discuss the price**, or you will get there (especially to one of the popular beaches) and find that they are sold out of that low price and your quote will be 50% more (it may be anyway).

Most Tico houses do not have **hot water** in the bathroom sinks (only in the showers) – you have to ask about this item.

When you **visit the beaches**, on either coast, you will find the weather is really hot – CR is only about 10 degrees north of the Equator, and the 100+ degree temperature with 90% humidity can be really stifling. I do recommend – in this instance only – that you get a room with air conditioning, although an overhead fan may do the job. Be very, very sure to cover yourself with sun tan oil – even though you "tan nicely" because the rays here are far more intense than you will realize, especially for youngsters.

When you **shop** at many of the larger independent stores you will find that you deal with a clerk, then your purchase is given to someone else who inspects the ticket and the product, to be sure you have the right purchase, and gives you a copy of the charge ticket, then you go to a cashier with your copy of the ticket and you pay, then you take that stamped ticket to the inspector person who will give you your item. Very secure and time consuming. Everyone smiles, however. The upscale department store Yamuni has five processes one goes through when making a purchase. It is fascinating to shop there.

Due to the crime (covered elsewhere) you will see an armed guard standing outside every large store and every bank in the country; he has strict orders not to smile and will be carrying a very strange-looking rifle/sawed–off-shotgun/pistol obviously made in Hungary or Mongolia. **Armed guards** are inside the stores as well, and also "floor attendants" who watch the customers. Most aisles have a uniformed young lady standing quietly in about the center, just looking for possible pilferers (what a savings could be made if surveillance monitors were placed throughout the store with one employee to watch the lot!). But these young women are always available to answer questions. And when you do they will take you to the item you are seeking.

For **fresh flowers** in the room stop at one of the *fincas* – flower farms on the mountain slopes among the coffee bean fields on the north side of the Central Valley where Calla Lilies and Birds of Paradise are about $.20 each. And while you are over there in the coffee growing area of Costa Rica, seek out the small-farm special coffee that will be stocked by the *pulperia* – it will have a special flavor.

Life's a Beach

And it really is in CR – there are 85 or so in this country, almost all on the Pacific side. When we talked of moving here most people automatically thought we would live at the beach. So many of the tourists who come in the millions head for the beach, and then do their other sightseeing from there. As anyone who has ever been here will tell you, the beaches in this country are beautiful, and there are dozens of them on the Pacific (preferred) and the Caribbean (fewer and less patronized) and not many people are at any one beach at any one time! Of course, the two or three most popular ones can be busy in season, but even then there are a dozen within a short drive that are not. At any time in the year (the temperature is about the same through the rainy and dry seasons) you can drive a few miles until you see a beach with not a soul in sight.

As I said earlier, the only thing we have against the beach life is that it is too hot. But, you may find the 85–110 temperature plus the high humidity is a relief from the cold of a northern winter. If lovely, sloping white beaches and a surf that can be from one foot to ten feet, and excellent accommodations from first class hotels down to the hostels that the kids fill each season, plus excellent dining – lots of seafood – and all kinds of other adventures awaiting – jungle rides and walks, horseback riding through jungles, fishing, snorkel and scuba, etc., etc. are your thing, then the beach is for you.

The two most visited spots in Costa Rica are the towns of

Manuel Antonio, and Tamarindo – about five hours from each other on the Pacific coast. Manuel Antonio is a national park half way down the Pacific coast where one can supposedly see hundreds of species of birds and animals, enjoy hours of trails through the jungle, sit and even swim in quiet, unpopulated small coves with undisturbed sand (if you have paid the fees), and shop next door in the tiny town with dozens of small tent shacks as well as the more upscale strip malls. The food is good too, just more expensive than most beaches because so many tourists go there. Toni and I took a couple of the trails, declining to pay $7.00 each to a guide with a telescope so we could maybe see the sloths and birds and monkeys that may or may not be hidden in the trees. In the few hours we hiked we didn't see a single tropical bird, animal, or insect. But the trails were steep and good exercise.

As in any place that is popular, the high rise condominiums, apartments and hotels are going up in Manuel Antonio as fast as the tourist numbers are increasing. It is a nice place to visit, but because of the swarms of tourists – and the resultant problems – I wouldn't want to live near there. It will have sewage disposal and pure water problems, as will the other beach places that are becoming high-end resort locations.

About 35 miles or so north up the beach from Manuel Antonio is the older beach community of Jaco. Frequented by both Tico and tourist, it has a large and growing development problem as well. It also has one of the highest crime rates in the country – drugs apparently got started, and with very few police to bother them, the crime just grew. My advice: get a report on the area before driving through it with your doors locked. Incidentally, Jaco also has a water problem in that the local government turned the local operation of the water system to the Federal government

(Instituto Nacional de Aqueductos AyA). The latest water figures show an average sized hotel had its bill increase from $58/month to $675/month and sometimes much higher. The water was shut off for the whole weekend in late July, 2007! The mayor has tried for five months to get some response from the government with no success, but now AyA is going to pay the community a visit and see if things can't get straightened out.

Another Jaco problem is the beach. An advertisement for the city in the on-line English newspaper *A.M. Costa Rica* suggested " … unless you are an experienced swimmer don't go into water above your knees …." because of the dangerous rip tide. And yet developers and realtors are actively promoting lots, condos, and homes in and around Jaco. Can you imagine a slogan "Buy at the beach but don't go near the water!" Also in the Jaco planning is a very large marina – 350 boats – to be built at the south end of the beach. There is talk of filling in areas and putting up shops and parking areas – "pave over paradise and put up a parking lot." Joni Mitchell had it right.

Also, as in every beach community – and elsewhere in CR – find out how they handle sewage and where they get their water, does it get any treatment, and can a person swim there?

However! The government – the CR Tourism Institute ICT – recently announced that signs will be put up at 31 beaches throughout the country (a little more than 1/3) warning of dangerous currents. Jaco and Tamarindo are two of the sites. Also, you should know that we have never seen a lifeguard at any beach in the country. There may be some somewhere, but I have never seen any.

The upscale village of Flamingo is about five more hours drive northwest up the coast from Jaco. It is just a few miles north of Tamarindo, and has a highly touted harbor for the yachts of the wealthy who live in palatial homes scattered throughout the hills above the small bay and inlet. It had its problems when the government shut the harbor marina construction down a year or so ago. It was based on some infraction that had been overlooked for years. But now they are getting started again with building a marina and creating docking slips. There is a fine beach, and just enough stores around to qualify the area as a village.

Other upscale resorts planned for that area will get competition in that department from a newcomer to the area. AOL founder Steve Case is planning to build – get this – an $800 million luxury beach resort complex on Cacique Point between the popular beaches Hermosa and Cocoa. With 263 hectares – a bit under 660 acres – he bought a whole peninsula! – he is planning three 5-star hotels, 120 Casitas, 60 private villas, 30 residences, an 18 hole golf course, and a tennis and fitness center labeled with the famous names of Andre and Stefi! One of the hotels will be the "One & Only" that in other places in the world, lists rooms starting at around $500 a night! Case has met with President Arias, touting the thousands of jobs that will be created. The corporation promises "low impact and low density, and that they have 'acquired' access to water." (Maybe Steve could tell the government where he "acquired" water and the government could buy some too!) Case says he will give $1 million to provide protection for the environment. (.002% of the total investment). The CR government overseeing agency SETENA, however, rejected the Cacique Point environmental-impact study, so it's back to the drawing board. We're waiting with baited breath to see what miracles Steve will come up with.

And even **he** has competition! One of the world's richest

people, Saudi royal family man Al-Walecd bin Talal Alsuad plans to put up two luxury hotels in the Papagayo area, and says he may just build an additional two or three more. Papagayo is a project directed by the Institute Costarricense de Tourism. No mention of water or electricity.

The very popular beach community of Tamarindo is a few miles south of Flamingo. Kids come for the surfing and adults for the sixty or so hotels, restaurants, shops, and services of all kinds. The funky little one-block-long community is popular with the locals, the young set, and is the second most popular tourist beach in the country! Its waters provide some very good surfing, and there are long, gently sloping beaches for swimming.

It has been recently touted as the fastest growing community in the world! More hotels, condos, luxury homes for sale or rent, golf courses, and commercial buildings are being built than many of the residents of the town believe the infrastructure will be able to handle – when it gets infrastructure! At the time of this writing in 2007 there is no sewage treatment plant, no water company, no zoning, one policeman, no density regulations, and most of the roads are not paved – nor do they have sidewalks!   It is really "something else" in the rainy season. They have a newly elected president of the Tamarindo Improvement Association that is working with the municipality of Santa Cruz, which oversees Tamarindo. The Santa Cruz mayor is providing assistance with their police, and there is the ncw "tourist police" as well as rural guards. And the town is drawing up zoning plans. The bureaucratic set up is that the municipality (Santa Cruz) will work with the National Institute for Housing and Urban Development (INVU) and those efforts will filter down to Tamarindo. Unfortunately, there is not enough money to do a real comprehensive planning for the future since municipalities only get about 2% of the total government spending, which is among the lowest in all Latin America. So they are starting out without enough money!

"Where is the water coming from and where is the sewage going to" is the rally cry among many of the businesses operating now as the town struggles to set up a council, get a police force and fire department going, trash collection system, and on and on. With allegedly 10,000 people coming in and out weekly during the high season, it is a busy little 1-street-1-block-long downtown. In this bureaucracy there are no zoning laws or restrictions on buying land for any purpose, so U.S. money is coming in, buying up a mountainside, and building right down to 50 meters of the half-way point between high and low tides – which is a national regulation, along with the requirement for having to get a concession to build on the next 150 meters. That the one-bedroom condo wealthy folks bought for $450K could run out of water, potable or otherwise, within five years doesn't seem to be anyone's worry. When we stayed at a modest motel near the beach last year **the water was rationed** – shut off for four hours during the day – and the signs said to **put all toilet waste paper in the disposal can and not in the toilet**! There is no municipal sewage system for the dozens of hotels, and the dozens more being built. If the town had the legal council today to authorize a sewage plant construction, and if it had the money, and if the bids were let out, and if a construction company was selected and approved by all the government agencies involved, it would be years before a plant would be in operation. In the meantime, the government has finally taken some notice and the Ministry of Health tested water in some of the sewage systems and found ".. a variety of contaminants 12 times higher than acceptable levels." Dr. Garcia (of the Health Ministry) said that there was a "very serious problem" but he was quick to point out that the study did not cover drinking water, only "**the sewage, that now runs into the ocean**"! (Where swimmers swim and surfers surf and nobody says a word). There was a recent full page advertisement appearing in *The Journal* (the English newspaper for western CR) for an upscale resort community to be built one kilometer away from the center of Tamarindo (only one of many ads for condos and homes). Rentals during the high season would be from $3,500 a week – now that's high end! The ad said they would have a "water treatment plant for waste water" but no mention of sewage treatment – in this country there is grey water and black water = waste and sewage. The fresh water is to come from "the municipality" (that is already rationing water?), and an independent regulated water supplier. Sounds like water will be trucked in. The ad appeared in June, 2007. A week later, however, there was an article in the paper that said the area would get water from Lake Arenal, which already supplies Guanacaste farmers through large canals, and which – after this drought season – now has a problem in that the water level is so low that the hydroelectric plant is producing less than the average amount of power. The plan seems to be to reroute some of the water and claim no one will have less water! There's logic for you. And this water is going for golf courses and Jacuzzis? Then, when visiting the Nicoya Peninsula recently, President Arias promised to provide beach development with water from Lake Arenal! This in the face of the fact that there are an estimated 35 tourism projects – hotels and luxury realty developments – planned for the next three years – some $2.1 billion (not counting Steve Case's project!). Water rationing is also already happening in the lovely and popular beach community of Hermosa. Well, sooner or later reality will set in.

With the dozens of high rises going up, the town of Tamarindo is just getting started! Without any sewage treatment plant, such septic systems as there are will soon be at the water table level. That will become saturated in a few years, but that's capitalism, folks. When we visited a few months ago one of the sub-contractors of a high rise building told me that raw sewage is already seeping into the estuaries that lead to the bay where the great surfing is! He will not let his children swim at the Tamarindo beaches. This town is a very popular place for *Norte Americanos.*

Some of the big real estate companies selling these luxury condos and homes sites are branches of U.S. firms – Remax and Century 21 among others. Some realty companies employ "boiler rooms" with banks of salesmen dialing up prospective U.S. buyers and giving a pitch for different projects throughout the country – they are always advertising for English-speaking sales people. Libera, about 45 minutes east of Tamarindo, is the largest city in the northwestern part of the country. It has a large and expanding airport as more and more international flights are scheduled here. One hundred thousand surfers came through this airport last year – the majority of them North Americans!

Tamarindo has very good restaurants, and you can still find reasonable accommodations if you know someone who can tell you of "that fabulous six room inn right on the beach for $65.00 a night in high season, with breakfast."

Of course, with the young surfing crowds come drugs, and with drugs comes crime, so there are some sore spots on the underbelly of this happy and bustling little community (as if the water and sewage problems weren't enough). Knowing the greed of builders, I would say that there will be $25K / yr. jobs in real estate sales for a few years more, but you can live on $10K as a beach-baby. Oh, and bring your golf clubs. It seems that every major U.S. hotel chain is building a resort and an 18 hole golf course within ten miles up and down the beach from Tamarindo. There are already fifteen golf courses in the Guanacaste Province (the most arid province in CR), most of them near the beaches. In a few years someone is sure to ask "Where the hell did all the water go?" The government planning always plays catch-up to reality in a developing country. They will start planning, zoning, and regulating growth just as soon as major builders start going broke, the infrastructure collapses, and/or some other major catastrophe occurs. It is always the way – wait till it happens then do something to prevent it from happening. We love this country and do hate to see the financial rapine that is going on that can only have disastrous results for the environment – and the environment **is** the country!

As I mentioned earlier, there are literally dozens and dozens of beaches on the Pacific side with no construction yet. This is where deep white sands stretch for a mile, where the jungle comes right down to the shore and where the people in the little village tucked in behind the palms are gentle and accommodating. Remember, the whole of the Caribbean and Pacific shores are open to public use. There is a caveat, however. There are many beaches where **the riptide is awesome** and you ALWAYS have to find out from the locals what the swimming and tide is like before you venture in.

If you want a different and more rural scene, take the ferry from Puntarenas over to the Nicoya Peninsula and drive around the southern end and up the coast. The roads are not the best, and I recommend a four wheel drive, but you will find a far more natural setting where the people are happy and friendly, not worried and concerned. As well as having an art colony, there is an internationally known community that has some of the most long-lived people in the world. Good air, simple foods, and a no-stress life will do it every time. There are some fine accommodations for tourists as well.

Finally, down the southern tip of the country is the city Golfito and the Osa Peninsula – "the as-yet-untamed Costa Rica." This area has been the last to receive attention as to roads, electricity, and similar infrastructure. To the north is the Talamanca Mountain region that is home to the Bribri Tribe, one of the six remaining indigenous tribes in the country, the others being Cabecor, Boruca, Huctare, Guaymie, and Terraba. Many of the tribes live deep in the jungle, miles from any road or even pathway. Many of those inhabitants have not left their tribal site in generations, speak their own language, and have their own customs and gods and shamans. The government is just now beginning to bring some of the "amenities of civilization" to these remote people – it is hoped to their betterment.

The area of the Osa Peninsula with its Corcovado National Park is one of the few remaining zones of Costa Rica available to visitors that is a totally wild and natural setting. Corcovado is about the size of New York's Central Park. The National Geographic called it the most biographically diverse place on the planet! And now the government says it has no more money to pay the salaries of the park guards.

Before the guards and scientists were hired just three years ago to protect the jaguars, wild peccaries and the dozens of other different wildlife, they were being hunted by poachers to foreseeable extinction. Now protected by the patrols, the animals are beginning to stabilize and the dense jungle has remained pristine. Thanks to the millions in grants from foundations and private citizens – who picked up the ball when the government said it could not fund the guard's salaries – the park is strongly recovering from the human depredations. But in this modern age of automatic weapons, the wildlife in this area has no chance once the human protection is gone.

The CR Nature Conservancy and other private institutions have agreed to fund the salaries for the remaining part of the year, but the government must pick up the funding again after that. As always in this beautiful country there is a money shortfall, and a government that doesn't know what to do about it, or has not the will.

The jungles around Golfito that sit on the deep gulf (tenth deepest in the world) are still pristine and are "developed" in but a few places. The United Fruit Company held sway there for fifty years, and their presence is marked by the town's buildings on stilts. The largest mangrove forest in CR is there, and Sir Francis Drake is supposed to have dropped anchor in the bay in 1579. Today, there is a well-known free trade zone there that many come to in order to buy things directly from the U.S. without the duty. That treasure is much more real than the one Drake is alleged to have buried in the Gulf sands.

This is the really great fishing area of Costa Rica, and one of the **best in the world** for large fish. And, some of the finest surfing is to be found also. The roads on the Osa Peninsula are really primitive and you must have a four wheel drive car to negotiate the rivers and the jungle trek. You should carry your own water and extra gasoline and food and even a bed roll if you perchance get stuck somewhere in a village with no inn and if you speak little Spanish! Every half dozen or so miles there are little villages on pristine beaches with a few gentle people about. When you are traveling in such a way be sure and observe the most stringent rules about dealing with strangers, locking your car doors and safeguarding everything when you hole up for the night. The remote areas of the peninsula have had some drug boats from Columbia come in to transfer their cargo.

A major problem yet to come for this pristine area is that only 16% of the 32.4 sq. km. of the maritime zone (beach area) has a zoning plan, and about 2000 concessions of all kinds have already been granted! There is illegal development according to a study done by the Comptroller's Office completed in 2006 (it only took six years). And without careful, dedicated planning for growth, problems for the ecosystem will happen. Already there is a nasty algae weed growing around some dive sites that gets a growth stimulation from the effluent of the small "civilization" that now exists there.

A real problem for this lovely environment is sure to happen because Presidente Arias supports the CR development authority's $1.2 million study for building a Southern Zone International Airport (a third one in this country the size of West Virginia?) right next to the most important wetlands in Central America, on the westernmost tip of the peninsula. And with it will come hotels, resorts, and commercial activity of all kinds. The government promises "strict management of solid and liquid waste, and fuel, according to current environmental standards" says a report in the *Tico Times*. As has been noted elsewhere, today's "current standards" are that 97% of the country dumps it's sewage into the rivers! Surely some responsible authority somewhere in the government will come to the understanding that this country has become a tourist Mecca only because of its natural beauty, the ecosystems, the flora and natural fauna, and the untamed wildlife. Surely they will understand that when that is compromised, tourism will decline. Surely, and without question. In these matters for this still-lovely country, **Less Is More**!

As for the wealthy traveler who takes the local airline NatureAir and flies to the small Golfito airstrip, he may be taken in a new four-wheel-drive Hummer to the modern, luxurious hotel/resort/spa/casino etc. looming out of the jungle. He will have a touch of American opulence in a wild setting for only $1,000 or so a night. The incongruity is striking. And sad.

The real development will get to this area in a few years, but for now, for the most part, it is still "truly Costa Rica." The Costa Rica of today is a lovely place to live, yes. So we enjoy the place and the pace, knowing that it will be less tranquil as "modernization" takes over. And before it can take its place as a small but industrialized nation, it will have severe growing pains – the processes of making all the water pure, of providing sewage systems, of creating adequate police and fire systems, a government that becomes more responsive, and on and on. Most expats know that, and we learn to maneuver around the problems while they are happening.

And we probably won't want to live here when it becomes sanitized.

.

202

Postscript

Well, my friend, that is our Costa Rica. We do love living here, with all the problems, faults, and consternations. If you adopt a Tico lifestyle and respect everything and everyone here, you can truly find peace and contentment, the aggravations becoming the adventures of life! I am sure you realized somewhere in the middle of this discourse that the anomalies of living here are just that – part of the landscape – and without them life would be a lot less interesting. If you come to stay you will gradually assume the attitude that living is not about being on time, or having things efficient and organized, or certainly not about making or even having money. You will take whatever steps you decide necessary to safeguard your property, health, and well-being. You will come to see that the momentary irritations only highlight the tranquility. For the next few years, at least, being here is ... *Pura Vida*!

Supplement II

Moving to Costa Rica

Because so many people have thought about moving here I thought to write a Supplement about how to do just that. The previous chapters have given both an insight into the lovely people, the government, and many of the problems one encounters in living here. But they all pale beside the pleasure of just being in this land so different from the place from which we came. Also, you may find some repetition in my noting this or that – just for emphasis.

Toni and I have lived happily and comfortably here for four years. In this Supplement I have amplified some of the areas of life to give you a better insight. I also go into the details about making a move. Throughout this book – reading about the problems as well as the details of living, I have tried to give to potential U.S. emigrants an understanding of exactly what it is like, it's people, the customs, and information about most of the facets of living in its towns and cities and the seaside areas. You will, I think, come to understand the cultural and functional differences that sometimes make it a challenge to embrace.

This Supplement is to tell you how to get started in the process, which can be convoluted and frustrating, as you must have guessed by now. You will learn what you will experience in moving here, and how to find what you want in a home, and where you want it. I have included in this Supplement much of the information and facts you should know when considering a move that means considerable change. My information comes from researching books, periodicals, the five English language newspapers in print and on-line, government publications, talking to expatriates and Costa Ricans, their organizations, and through living in and traveling through this lovely land.

The Beginning

When my wife Toni and I thought to make a move from the U.S., it was because we wanted to live in a place where we could afford not to have to *do* anything, being on a small fixed income, and find a place where we could just *be*. We first thought of Costa Rica as a nice little place that exports coffee and is apparently quiet, but we knew little else. I certainly was not aware that there are almost 60,000 United States, Canadian and European expatriates living here. I had heard that hundreds, if not thousands, of U.S. citizens move here every year because of the climate, the beauty, the people, a relaxed democracy, and the inexpensive cost of living.

In the previous chapters you had many a glimpse into the problems this growing country is facing! There are, however, many very good reasons to be here. CR is a "socialized democracy" with a delightful climate of around 70 degrees in the winter and up to 80 degrees in the summer, with evenings cooling to 60 (in the mountain areas); a public transportation system that will take you anywhere you want to go; a country of exceptional natural beauty; very inexpensive modern housing, where you can be very comfortable on an income of $2000 per month. Now, that ought to be enough to sway most people! And most important, CR is a place where the people still like North Americans and they are among the most polite, kind and friendly people you will find anywhere.

In this Supplement I deal with telling you exactly how to come here as a retiree seeking *Pensionado* Status, and the slightly higher financial requirements for the *Rentista* Status. (I do not deal with the more complex requirements of the Investor Status, nor the Temporary Residency Permits for students, foreign firm employees, etc.) You will learn what is required to live among these decent descendents of ancient Natives, English, Jamaicans, Dutch, and yes, even *Norte Americanos*, among others. As you will have learned from the other chapters in this book, all is not peaches and cream. This is a developing country, albeit the most advanced in Central America, and it does have its challenges, so adapting to this culture may not be for everyone. .

In deciding to make a major change in our lives, and after hearing about Costa Rica, Toni and I read through the few travel books on this country, and the one book available about actually making the move proved to be outdated. That book, *Living Overseas, Costa Rica,* by Robert Johnson, published by Living Overseas Books, Naples, FL, 2000, may have been updated by this time. It has much information that a prospective resident should have. However, this country is growing and changing so rapidly that often last year's information may no longer be valid.

As I noted in the beginning of this book, when we arrived, almost from the minute we got off the plane we found that a great deal of the information we had read about the people, their habits, things you need to have, to do, and to be prepared for, were out of date, incomplete, or inaccurate. There was not much help for us to know what we should do the first morning Toni and I woke up in our hotel room in San Jose, or subsequently through the next weeks of trying to find a home, and what to do when we found one, and the small difficulties of moving to a developing foreign country.

When we decided to make this move from our home in New Mexico, our friends and family asked many times "Why do you want to move to Central America?" The answer we gave may strike a chord.

Why Did We Move?

Basically, our reason was economic. We could no longer afford to live in our rented home in Santa Fe, New Mexico, admittedly one of the most expensive places in the U.S. Living almost anywhere else, however, either Toni or I would have to work since I had no corporate retirement pension, nor had I been prudent in my younger years and dutifully "saved up a bundle for my old age." I am one of the mavericks who spent his money as he made it and enjoyed every minute of living! After the 2000 stock market romp deflated the little I had stored away, all I had for certain was a modest fixed income and a little savings. I was 81 years old, and my wife 54 – a fairly unusual situation you will agree. We had been married for two years and wanted to live where neither of us had to work so we can spend the rest of my life being together.

One evening, in late September, after going over our finances, Toni looked at me and said "What are we going to do? We really can't afford to live here anymore!" And we surely didn't want to drop in on any of our children and say "Hi, we're here to stay!"

So, we started looking. We considered a rural village in New Mexico or Arkansas or some other low-cost area, but we were too used to the variety of life to squirrel ourselves away in some forgotten tiny community. We thought about Ireland and Italy, but the cost of living there today is higher than one would think. We looked carefully at Mexico – certainly inexpensive to live – and were offered a lovely home near Puerto Vallarta free for 6 months, but Mexico did not personally appeal to us.

Someone, at some time, had mentioned Costa Rica as a wonderful country, so we started asking friends and acquaintances if they had heard anything about it. Everything we heard in reply was "great country, great beaches, really cheap to live, excellent health system," and more. The next Friday afternoon we went to Borders Bookstore and sat down on the floor by the Central America section and read through the few travel books on this country. Very little we read was a deterrent. The place seemed just right for us – a place where we could live on my income (the legal Costa Rican government requirement is a guaranteed income of $600 per month) and be together without either of us having to work. Also, a country where there seemed to be unlimited possibilities, for work if one wished, but for us to expand our life and live without having to do anything; a new country to meld into and find the ease and contentment denied by the struggle to exist comfortably in the U.S., with its high standard/cost of living.

Your reasons may be economic, or it may be that you want to find a country where the people are friendly, very polite, and live with personal dignity, regardless of their station in life; where one rarely sees or hears rudeness of one to another, where family is revered and children are loved. It may be that you want to move to a developing country where economic opportunity seems unlimited and where there are many small business areas where one could make a living with little investment. Or, you may want to move to live in a country where you could spend every week of the year seeing a different scenic tropical wonderland; where the lovely beaches are just a few hours away from anywhere in the country. You may be simply tired of having to put up with the vagaries of the weather, the cold and snow and sleet, and want to spend your days in a climate of warm days, gentle breezes, and cool nights. Or, you may want to find a democratic society that seems to be the way the U.S. was 40 years ago – few regulations, each person responsible for his or her own actions.

Back to the bookstore. Having spent the afternoon going through the few travel books – I found *Insight Guides, Costa Rica,* published in London, to be the most comprehensive on the history and culture, as well as travel tips; but it contained dated statistical information. We walked to nearby Pranzo's, our favorite restaurant, and sat down at the bar. We looked at each other, and Toni said "Let's do it!" I turned on my stool and we shook hands, which made it irrevocable. We were going.

Six weeks after that Friday night handshake we flew into San Jose, arriving at 9:00 o'clock at night with two carry-on bags and two 50 lb. (maximum allowed) large suitcases of clothes each, with 23 boxes of books and mementos to follow. We had sold everything we owned at an estate sale. We had the telephone number of a recommended immigration attorney, and that of a customs agent to whom we had spoken several times in preparing for our move. The serendipitous events that led us to the lovely home in which we first lived, and the even more magical circumstances that led us to our present beautiful home, are testament to the wonderful people of this land, and to my belief that if you just joyfully embrace your venture, what ever it is, and be open for what will come, you will find what you desire.

If you find yourself working too hard to make ends meet and if you have an income of $2000 a month (the travel books say a couple can live on $1000 a month, but that's impossible), then consider making a change – it can be done!

How It's Done

Once you put out the word you are moving to Costa Rica (CR) you will find people you didn't know calling and telling you how wonderful it is. You will hear from friends who know people who live there, and from acquaintances that have just visited. People you barely know will call and say, "I hear you are moving to Costa Rica, well, you MUST call so and so, they live there at such and such, and would love to steer you in the right direction." Not to mention the people who will call and say they are going there for a vacation this year, and "... be sure and give us your phone number when you get there so we can get together!" Also, almost everyone will assume you are going to live "at the beach" because so many people come here to visit in the winter and stay at one of the dozens of fine beaches on the Pacific side.

As noted earlier, we decided we did not want to live at the seaside. We wanted mountains and views, and to be among the local people. Living in a city was also out for us. We wanted a quiet, peaceful lifestyle among the Tico population, perhaps near some North Americans, but certainly not in an American enclave. Costa Rica literally has all life styles available – all. You can find a place that fits your income at the beaches, in the city, the suburbs, and the rural countryside. You can live among English-speaking Canadians, North Americans, British, and people of other European countries; you can find a mixture of cultural backgrounds in almost every populated area of the country. You can even live in the tropical jungle among the monkeys and exotic birds, if that is your wont. You can find a new little house in a village to rent for $400 a month, or a mansion with a pool for $3,000 a month. You can buy a nice, new 2-bedroom and 2-bath house for $95,000, or a 4-bedroom, 4-bath house, with an office, a sun room, Jacuzzi, and a swimming pool for $450,000 – at the beach or in the mountains. Or, you can rent or buy a home costing in the millions! This country has anything you want, where you want it.

Be assured, the temperature is splendid. The climate, however, is really different. You must quickly get used to a season of rain every day for six months, and then dry for six months. And then there are the ten "mini-climates" in the country. The climate even varies from town to town in the Central Valley and elsewhere.

So, first you decide you are seriously thinking about moving here on a permanent basis. We were chided by friends who asked "Have you ever been to that country?" We replied "No, but from all we've heard, it's a great place, so why spend the money and go and find out what we have already been told!" This approach may be naïve, I guess, but it proved to be the correct one for us. When we first called the immigration attorney mentioned above, who speaks good English, he asked "When were you last here?" When I replied, "Well, we have never been to your country," he paused and said, "You know, when you go to a shoe store to buy some shoes you usually try on a pair before you buy!"

For everyone else I will say, yes, if you are planning to become a permanent resident, **visit the country first** — try the shoe on to be sure it fits. Take some time to get a feel for the people, the lifestyle, the geography; and spend some time finding out about the many towns and cities, near and far from San Jose, the capital. It will make your move easier if you know the area where you would like to live, and know that you will be able to find something perfect in that area. This section, therefore, is developed to aid you as you first go to CR as a tourist, then come back to your home and, with the decision made, start the emigrating process.

It may all seem confusing and even inexplicable at the start — Alajela, Escazu, Heredia, Santa Ana, Cartaqa, San Jose (about the only city you may know of because it is the capital), the beach areas of Puntarenos, Flamingo, Tamarindo, Puerto Viejo, Quepos, and more. Going to Costa Rica to visit as a tourist is very different from making a visit with the intention to move here.

Also, be assured that when you are estimating costs for this adventure of a lifetime, you will probably spend much more than any quotation you have been given, all along the way, from shipping to customs, to legal fees, and everything else in the move.

Beginning the Process

Please note that the following sections detail the process required in finding a home in the Central Valley, and in the surrounding mountains — our experience. Be assured, however, that in finding a home in the many beach communities the process is the same. While the climate may vary from area to area, the people and customs do not.

So, you have decided. You are most seriously considering moving to Costa Rica. You have first prudently decided to visit the country for at least two or three weeks, to drive around or first be driven around (recommended) and get an understanding of the culture and the people, and most important, get an idea of where you want to live.

To visit Costa Rica as a tourist you are required to have a U.S. Passport. It is needed to enter the country, and you will use it when you stop at a hotel and want to register, change Traveler's Checks at a bank, and many other circumstances. You should also have a U.S. drivers license as a second identification. And, if you plan to drive here it might be nice to have an international driver's license, but you really don't need one. You won't get hauled in if you are stopped without one – as long as you have your valid U.S. license.

By the way, **DO** purchase an English-Spanish Dictionary a few weeks before your trip and study it! Learn the common phrases and how to say "I," "we," "you," "eat," "buy," "change," etc. etc. We have found that very few people speak English outside the major hotels and major tourists places.

The following suggestions are made with the understanding that you area going to make a visit first. So, try and find a travel agent that has visited CR! Second best, find someone who has visited here. Talk to them about places, where they have been, etc. And get a travel book with a map so you can follow what they are talking about. Then, have the travel agent book your flight, the hotel where you will first stay in San Jose (the Irazu on the western edge of San Jose is where we stayed), and perhaps a tour or two of the most desirable tourist areas to see after reading the travel books – if you want to do a little tourist travel. Plan your trip for the lifestyle you want to have when you move here – where you want to live – Mountain, Seashore, Village, City, or private enclave, condominium, house, high rise apartment, or beachside mountaintop! For the beach area there is the Pacific side – where most of the fine beaches are and where there are the most homes available for rent and sale – and the Caribbean side, where there is the small city Limon but far fewer beaches (and it is HOTTER!). The best of the Caribbean beaches are to be found south of Limon near the Panama border. Puerto Viejo is a charming town with great beaches.

For the mountains you can go almost all the way northwest and southeast. But if you want to stay near the Central Valley – the San Jose area – you should visit the towns in the hills north and south, east and west of the capital city. For really rural living there are small towns and villages from 4000 to 7000 feet all around San Jose. However, it may be somewhat more difficult to find the home of your dreams in these more remote places, unless you are seeking a more upscale dwelling. A list of my desirable towns is included in the preceding chapters.

When you arrive you may want to stay the first few nights at a Marriott or Best Western (Irazu) or similar U.S. chain hotel in San Jose – they are both high quality and inexpensive by U.S. standards. However, there are also several excellent, first class small hotels in downtown San Jose that will immediately immerse you in this country. They won't be very costly, they will be charming, and the food will be excellent in their restaurants.

The first few days you are in or near San Jose in your hotel just getting the feel of things, you will have to **find a bilingual guide**. You can find him or her through the *Tico Times* (the English language newspaper available at the stands in the hotel, nearby supermarkets, etc.) or through asking your desk clerk at the hotel. (As a side note, you can write for a *Tico Times* to be mailed to you).

The guide you find will both be able to recommend tours to the scenic sights (if you are determined to see some first), and will also be able to drive you to the various communities and areas mentioned in the book so you can get a feel for those communities and get an understanding of what it will mean to live in one. Guides recommended by your concierge at the hotel, as well as those advertising their services, will most likely be very responsible and will take you, with good to excellent English, through the process of traveling about the country. Guides who are recommended by the hotel and other responsible sites have to go to the "tourism university" here and get a certificate before they can hang out a shingle, so they **will** be good.

Study a map of CR. Note all the smaller cities and towns around San Jose, and note the principal beach communities where there are significant towns and growth, and **ask your guide any questions you have**. But be assured that he will be prejudiced in favor of the area in which he lives. If you have decided before you leave you want to live at the beach, then you can spend a week or so seeing all of the beaches and the MANY developments going up.   After finding the area you want, you can plan to come back, settle in at a temporary apartment or *aparthotel*, and search out the place of your dreams. Once your area is selected on this trip you can do a little sightseeing – a trip to Arenal (the volcano that fires off almost nightly) and a few other great scenic places.

Take note of the several fine beach areas, having asked your travel agent about them, and make sure your visit is scheduled to go to each of the areas you want may want to live – beach, mountains, villages, etc.

I do not suggest you rent a car and start touring the country. The driving here is different at best, especially once you get outside

San Jose; and since there are no streets named in any town outside the main cities (and not all in the cities) it is difficult to find your way around. Good Spanish is needed once you leave San Jose if you are traveling on your own. The very best way to see the area all around San Jose, if you are thinking about living in the Central Valley area and not at one of the beaches, is to tell your guide where you want to go and point it out on the map. He should have a car not more than 5 or so years old!

The guide will cost from $50 to $70 a day, possibly with the cost of gas added ($2.50 or more a liter). To see the whole area around San Jose, and to get to the beaches as well, will take a couple of weeks so you should negotiate with the guide for a package deal that will lower the daily fee. Note: if you hire a guide with whom you are dissatisfied, thank him or her, and find another. Pay at the end of each day. Do not run up a tab or you will find "other costs" he or she "forgot to mention." Remember, you will need compatibility as you roam around a new country for a few weeks asking questions.

If you are disposed to settle at one of the beach areas – the Pacific side is much preferred – then you will simply need to visit them to find the best beach town for you. It will take only a few hours to drive to Puntarenas, and then branch out from there. It will take around four hours to drive up to the north beach areas of Flamingo and Taramindo from Puntarenas, or down to the middle CR area of Jaco, Manuel Antonio, and Quepos. When you think of the beaches and the small towns near them, ask about the climate in the summer and the winter in each location. You might not like a fairly high temperature in the sun with only a light breeze in the summer, and may not want to deal with a rainy season of several months.

Actually, most locals say that in the Central Valley the "rainy season" means it will rain hard for about 2 hours every day in the early afternoon. Hard rain here can mean a real deluge! The mornings are sunny and warm – 70 degrees – and the evenings are cool. However, sometimes it rains a LOT; hard rain all day. You will note that I have not mentioned much about the Caribbean side, and the city of Limon. From what we have come to understand, living at the Pacific side is much more preferable for many reasons, milder climate among them. Keep in mind that CR is a small country about the size of West Virginia and one can drive to either the Pacific coast or the Caribbean coast in about 2 hours from San Jose, or get to either coast by bus in 3 hours (and around $3.50).

So, now you have a map, you have interviewed and selected a guide or rented a car, and selected the areas you want to visit. If you are renting a car to drive yourself, you have my admiration. The cost will be from $40 to $80 per day, the latter being closer to the mark because it will include insurance. The rental car man may tell you it is only $35 or $45 per day, but when he adds on the insurance you will see another $25 - $35 added. It is possible, however, to rent an older 4-wheel drive jeep or similar vehicle for from $150 per week, insurance added. I suggest, because of the country roads you may wish to travel, that a 4-wheel drive is the best option. But you may change your mind after reading the chapter in this book where I cover the challenges of driving in Costa Rica. Do yourself a favor and first plan to spend at least the first few days driving about with a guide, and then consider renting a car after you have seen what the driving situation is like.

Just to get the feel of the city, see San Jose for a day or two. Schedule a tour to the Theatro Central, the Gold Museum, the National Art Museum and more. And especially visit the Central Market that has been bustling since the 1800's. It is an extraordinary place and you will see just about anything you could want offered in the hundreds of little shops packed in side by side. You will see every kind of produce grown on the planet. Exceptional fish and meat markets, herb stalls, and stalls offering anything one could want for a household. It reminds me of the famous bazaar in Cairo! In addition, for two blocks around the market every sidewalk has stalls packed together, called *chinamos*, offering more of the same. This area will certainly let you know that you are indeed in a foreign country. It should be noted that the city is now considering banning those sidewalk stalls that have been there for a century, so things may be a bit different by the time you get here.

Also, see the downtown activity in other areas of San Jose that will show you different sides of the culture here and let you know how you feel about city living, or living on the outskirts of a large city of over two million people. San Jose is truly bustling, with buildings that range from ancient to ultra modern. The streets are narrower than you will be used to, and the people, automobile, and bus congestion will be very severe most of the time during the day. I cannot see how the city can absorb any more vehicles – which it will surely have to in the next years.

An interesting aspect to the city and it's traffic is the dozens of "entrepreneurs" – those men and women who walk between lines of cars and busses stopped at a light or intersection selling everything from cell phones, to accessories, little bags of coconut water, candy, all kinds of food, umbrellas, and more (see the picture on page 170!).

What makes San Jose different, and it is the same in all

Costa Rican cities, one will find a lovely house situated between large office buildings, and find a small exclusive shop next to a lovely home next to an office building. The city "just grew." As previously detailed, all the streets are numbered *Avenidas* and *Calles*. However, many times the numbers are not on any building (they do not use street signposts) and you have to estimate where you are. Most of the streets are one-way as well. Makes for confusion, but when you do find the place you are looking for, you will break out with "There it is! There it is!" and get a sense of having triumphed over the obfuscation.

After "enjoying" the bustle of San Jose, visit the several outlying smaller communities in the Central Valley – on the south mountain side Escazu, Santa Ana, and Cuidad Colon; on the north mountain side there is Heredia, Santa Domingo, Santa Barbara, Barva, San Rafeal; on the east end of the Central Valley is Cartago, and on the west end of the Central Valley there is Alajuela, Grecia, and San Ramon. You need to travel around in these small cities and villages if you plan to live other than at the seaside.

Even if you do plan a seaside home, you might just have your guide drive you to the areas and communities around San Jose mentioned in the above paragraph for a few days, just to get a feel for them, and then head west, north, or south (in that order) for the best beaches, and spend your time at the three areas mentioned above – Puntarenas, the most populated, and directly west of San Jose – a little over 2 hours away; Flamingo and Tamarindo, 3 ½ more hours farther up in the northwest part of CR; and Quepos, to the southeast, a 4 or 5 hour trip. There are other areas such as Golfito – 7 hours - in the far south, where you can get a ferry to the Peninsula de Osa, where there are many fine beaches and small towns, but the area is far more rural and without many amenities.

If you decide to leave your hotel and establish a base in one of the surrounding communities you will certainly hear about the dozens of Bed & Breakfasts (B&Bs) that abound in and around San Jose. There are also *aparthotels* – convenient lodgings that are exactly what the name portends – you get a living room, kitchen and bedroom (and breakfast) for from $40 - $80 a day depending on where it is and the quality level. Some are listed in the *Tico Times*, or you can ask the concierge at the hotel. Also, your guide will know of several. B&B's are another story. Many are available and they range from $30 to $80 a day. The quality usually matches the price, although many of the less expensive ones will be in a small town or rural area, and they can be a lovely place to stay. To find a good one you must ask more than one tour guide, hotel desk or concierge as each will have a friend in the business and will try to steer you their way. If you want to set up in a B&B and travel out of that place for a few days or a week or so, then make sure you visit a few before making your selection. No need to be shy about thanking and leaving a most solicitous manager or homeowner – they expect people to look first and decide later.

Another suggestion the travel books offer is to find a Tico family and live with them for a few weeks (to me just a homey B&B). One advantage touted is that you may learn some Spanish, having to speak it every day. The family does it to make a few extra *colones*. However, if you speak little or no Spanish, I think you will find it most frustrating to try to communicate and understand a reply. If the family is bi-lingual, splendid. Other than that I would rely on my bi-lingual tour guide. Besides, if you are going to travel about all day, or take overnight trips to some areas, you won't be getting much use out of the B&B except as a place to keep your gear.

Knowing in advance we wanted to live outside a city, in a rural area, preferably up in the mountains, we located in an *aparthotel* in Santa Ana, a small city six miles southwest of San Jose - $70 / day without tax (since we paid in cash – one of the ways the Ticos get around paying taxes) and including breakfast. We took day trips and came home at night and prepared dinner from the fresh foods purchased at the small local *pulperia* (the little grocery stores that are in every single community in CR). They have something of everything – you will find the freshest fruits and vegetables you can image.

When you settle in at an *aparthotel* (my recommendation), and talk to your guide and ask about the various areas you want to see, he will have his preference. If he lives in a particular town you can be sure he will tell you it is the best place to live in Costa Rica! There is great local pride for one's home area here. But, you should insist that you want to be driven through all the various areas and communities you have selected to see. You will find that local pride coming through when you suggest a place to see and your guide insists "It is not for you" simply because he does not live there. Insist. Then, after a week of visiting the several communities you will certainly have an idea of the various places, and each will indeed have its own character – even villages and towns two miles apart can seem to be very different here.

You may think, after finding you are becoming enthusiastic about moving to this lovely place, that you had "better search out a place right away because it may be gone when you come back to live." Don't worry, the place you want will be there later. Costa Rica is "developing." You will see growth and construction and many, many *Se Vende* (for sale) and *Se Acquila* (for rent) signs everywhere you go. When there is growth in a country, there is also a great deal of movement, and places become available every day. Just for now, find the area in which you want to live, mark it on the map, write out "on the west side of ......", "toward the south of the village of .....", etc. Know where you will be comfortable, then go back home with the certain knowledge you will find the perfect place for you when you come back to stay. Also, we know of U.S. couples who are spending from three to six months in an *aparthotel* so they can learn everything possible about the area they are considering, including finding those homes not listed in a newspaper or with any real estate agent. As mentioned elsewhere, you find those just by asking around the neighborhood.

We discovered that one should take at least two to three weeks traveling through the areas – city, suburban, rural, and seaside – decide on the area or town where you want to live, then, if you have decided to move here, you can return home and begin the immigration process. I personally believe that you will be able to find several perfectly suitable homes, so it would not be necessary to put deposits on a place to hold it. Also, we know of couples who have first rented an apartment for six months in order to roam throughout an area of interest. If you are planning first to live in an apartment and intend to pursue buying a house when you are here, there will be many, many apartments in all price ranges waiting for you.

It will be very advantageous for you if, during your stay in the San Jose area, you visit the Association of Residents of Costa Rica – ARCR – and tell them of your interest in moving to this country (more about this below). They will be most helpful in giving you a lot of information about what one needs to do. They will even suggest you join ARCR then and there, but this is not necessary until you come back to start living here. However, it might be helpful, and give you a little more confidence in what you are planning, to talk to one of their attorneys about your possible move. He or she can give you all the details.

By this time, after a few weeks in CR, I am assuming you either love the place or have decided it is not for you. If my former assumption is correct, you are ready to start the process, and here is where the excitement begins! Throughout the whole procedure developed below you must keep in mind that you are dealing with another country – a "Developing Country" – whose culture is different and things will NOT always work smoothly. Basically, the glitches will be small for CR, but then, you are used to American technology that makes most things go quickly, and you must know that they probably will not be quick here. We know of Americans who recently moved here who "can't understand why 'these people' don't just get more efficient!" My answer is that if they wanted technology they should have stayed home.

First Things First

You are now back home after having spent some time in CR and you have decided to move there. Before proceeding further I want to note a suggestion we were given, and which is written in all the travel books. You must find a good Immigration Attorney specialist who is recommended by someone you know and trust. This is an absolute "must." As in any foreign country there is a specific, exact process that must be followed. Also, some simple regulations change monthly, and your attorney must be conversant with all these changes. Should you ignore a seemingly unnecessary step, or do one out of sequence, the process may stop, you may forfeit or even have your application ended.

There are not-so-honest and not-so-capable lawyers in Costa Rica, as in every country – industrial, developing or not – who will both over-charge and not do the correct legal work for you. Initially this did happen in our case, despite having a recommendation.

We did, however, find the answer to getting a good, fair-charging attorney through ARCR. That second attorney was excellent. We were amazed, as was our attorney, that our application for residency permit was approved six weeks after it was submitted. We know people who have waited two years for *Rentista* permits.

I suggest that the FIRST thing you do from the U.S. is to contact ARCR if you did not visit them when in CR. If you stopped in to talk to them when in CR, call them and remind them of your visit, stating what your plans are now, that you will need an Immigration Attorney (IA) who will handle your immigration for you, and also, if need be, act for you in cases of leasing or buying property. When you talk to ARCR on the phone they will give you the name and telephone number of a competent attorney in their building (there are sixteen attorneys with offices there) who handles immigration cases and a time to call him or her. When you arrive in CR that attorney will also be able to guide you in the basics of setting up bank accounts, a lease for a house or apartment, and steer you through the various civil requirements that abound. Their attorneys specialize in immigration matters and the attorney recommended to you by ARCR will be able to handle all your requirements. Also, they are used to dealing with *Norte Americanos* who want everything done yesterday!

Even from your living room in the U.S. your IA will advise you on all aspects of the type of immigration status you are discussing, about taxes, renting, starting a company, purchasing property, etc. The IA will fax or email you a detailed list of everything you will need to do. **You should follow his or her advice and direction exactly!** You may find, as we did, that the people working at the various consulates in the U.S. may not be up-to-date in the required procedures, or may tend to overlook a detail here and there which will indeed throw the process off track.

An aside: Before you call, be sure you check with your telephone long distance carrier as to the cost per minute of calling Costs Rica from your home. Check the cost and double-check it. Possibly you should go on the internet to find the lowest cost carrier to Central America. We had checked with our carrier (Sprint) who told us – over the phone, nothing in writing – that our cost would be $.30 a minute. Fine. Eight weeks later, after we had arrived here, our bill came and we found we were charged $4.99 per minute on one call, $10.41 per minute on another, and $7.10 per minute on yet another call!! All calls were made to our attorney in San Jose, and all during the day. It is one of the finer points of American business that we found overcharges and double charges by almost every company with whom we dealt in closing out accounts in the U.S. Corporate integrity does slide beneath profit.

Now you have established communication with an attorney. The next person you will need is a Customs Broker (CB) in Costa Rica. Your IA will certainly know a reputable broker and will refer you to him. You will need to talk to the CB over the phone as well. He will tell you how to label your boxes, and how CR customs works, and how delivery of your goods is affected.

You will need to call the Costa Rica Consulate that has the responsibility for your state. There are only 10 CR Consulates in the U.S and each is responsible for several states. No matter how insistent the CR consulate person is on the telephone that you do not need this or that form or do not need to provided this or that information (after your IA has told you it must be provided) thank the person, then go ahead and get the information anyway. You will probably need it.

Allow several weeks to get all the information. It can take from 7 – 10 days for a CR Consulate to stamp a form and send it back to you. Plus, it is always possible that the form you sent to them "was not received," "cannot be immediately located," or "will have to be reviewed." Just bureaucratic stumbling consistent with any government anywhere. Indeed, you can probably expect delays – protestations from a U.S. agency from whom you are requesting information or a form, as well as the CR consulate, when you are trying to get birth certificates, a passport, a declaration that you have the required income, etc. With all the government concerns extant in the U.S. about travelers, expect delays. When asked by a government agency "Why do you want to go to Costa Rica," I always replied, "Just going to visit for a while and I want to be prepared if I want to stay beyond the tourist visa limit," or I made a similar disclaimer to avoid further questioning. This was true because it was possible that we could arrive here and find we did not like the culture as a place to reside permanently.

Once you have started the Residency Permit procedure, you should then contact a local Freight Forwarding Agent (FFA). The type of items you take will greatly affect the cost of shipping, the CR Customs fees, and the cost of receiving them. This means you must decide in general what items you will ship and how they will be packed. Reasonably accurate planning will need to be done.

Every city has an FFA. They will ship your goods out of

the country. If you don't know of one, look in the Yellow Pages and call a few. Or, ask a local business that exports or imports for a recommendation. When you talk to them you should be able to tell them approximately how many boxes you are shipping, general contents, estimated value, and general weight. Of course, not having packed up yet, you will have to guesstimate what your shipping weight, hence costs, will be. Use this figure to get an estimate of costs. Get estimates from two or more brokers, always asking how the goods will be shipped. Obviously, air freight will be faster but costs much more. You will find that there will be differences in charges – even by two brokers in the same city. You should ask how the goods will be shipped, and by what route! You should not be surprised that a FFA will often take the longer way to ship goods to CR because it makes more commission – larger cost, more profit. So, ask the FFA to give you a guaranteed rate with a plus or minus percentage! We were told that our goods would be trucked from Albuquerque to Houston, then shipped by boat from there to CR. We were given an estimate on this routing. Our goods were actually shipped by truck to Miami, then shipped in two different cargoes on two different boats to CR. Longer distance, more handling, more profit for the FFA. Our final cost was **almost double** the estimates given by our FFA and by the IA.

As noted above you will need a Costa Rica Customs Broker – CB – to receive the goods being shipped to that country. You can, initially, give him the same weights and number of boxes and the general contents given to the FFA so as to get your general cost. Unfortunately, I would guess that no matter how detailed your list and how carefully accurate your weight estimate and the duties on your goods when you finally are ready to ship, it will cost you considerably more than the estimates by the FFA and your CB.

You now have (1) contacted ARCR and also talked to the recommended Immigration Attorney by telephone and by emails in Costa Rice to get general advice on moving here, and have received exact information about all the steps you need to take to forward the process. Your IA will give you the exact cost he will charge. He will include his fees and all government fees. Our IA charge was $1,200.00 for both Toni and I. The primary (myself) resident charge was $700, and secondary (Toni) resident fee was $500. This included the lawyer's fees and the government charge of $100 each that is collected in case the government ever has to put you on a plane and send you back to the U.S.! Your charges may be more because the fees may have increased, but they should reasonably be within this range. (2) You have contacted by telephone and email a Customs Broker who has given you – via fax or email – exactly how he will proceed and what will happen once your goods shipment has reached Costa Rica, and has given you his estimate of the costs. (3) You have contacted by telephone and visited a local Freight Forwarding Agent and have all the details about your shipment, the approximate weight and cost and the manner and route it will be shipped. (4) You have completed all the 10 - 12 steps necessary to get your Residence Status Application. The only thing you have yet to do is visit the CR Consulate that handles your state and present your paperwork for their approval and acceptance. You can do this any time before you leave, or you can do it the day you leave. Remember, however, it must be done when you are in the U.S. If you wait until you have gone to CR you will have to return to the U.S. – you must deal with your local CR Consulate **in the U.S.**, not in CR.

Packing Up

Now comes the process of selecting out everything you will want to take with you, what you want to give to friends and relatives, what you want to sell, and what you may want to store for the future – either to have shipped to you later or against the time you may want to return to the U.S. For advice on what to take read the list in the back of this book. Follow the list as you wish, but it will save you much grief later on in trying to shop around to find that small item you decided against, but that you need in CR.

If you plan to send some of your furnishings to relatives to store for you, or if you plan to sell everything except what you have given away or are taking with you, it will take you some time to select the items you want to ship to CR, and getting the right size boxes to pack them in. I recommend you buy new boxes from your local box distributor, or Office Depot or similar store. You should ship your goods in 12X12X12 or 12X12X15 because of the weight and ease of handling. Of course a few boxes may have to be larger, depending on what you are shipping. **Do not** gather up used liquor or small appliance boxes, or boxes you get out of some dumpster. They will definitely confuse the CR customs people, no matter how you label them, and you will likely have everything delayed in customs while every single box is opened for content evaluation – which in turn will possibly mean a higher tax. Plus, your boxes could be misplaced or confused with someone else's shipment.

There are two ways to look at your emigration. (A) Make a clean sweep – sell everything through an Estate Sale and give to relatives and friends the mementos you don't want to take with you. (B) Give to relatives to store for you those items of furniture, books, linens, etc. you just don't want to sell (or to have as a "backstop" in case you may want to return to the U.S. to live at some point). We chose the former for the reasons given above. What you take with you is one of the main purposes of this section. You will find that no matter how thoughtfully and carefully you plan, when you arrive here you will find many little things you "should have brought with you." I will guarantee that if you know people who live in CR and you announce your intention to visit or move, you will have instant exclamations of "Oh, will you please buy – a small appliance, face cream, a magazine (and virtually anything available in the States and not easily available here) – and stuff it in your suitcase for us!"

In packing you do have limits. On the aircraft you can take two (2) carry-on bags and check two (2) bags of any size. However, your weight limit is now down to fifty (50) pounds when flying in the U.S., and fifty (50) pounds when taking an international flight! Remember – if you load your suitcases to more than 50 lbs. you will pay a high tariff! This could be up to $75.00 per bag. But then, it may be worth it to you if you are taking expensive small appliances, etc. Costa Rica customs do not tax any item you have in your carry-on bags or in suitcases you have checked. Of course, you can check a fifth bag and just pay the extra charge. It may be worth it. We had different charges quoted by the same airline every time we talked to someone different as to the extra charges, so check the extra cost more than once. Re-read the chapters about the housing in this country to get an understanding of what you will need. Select the clothes you will want in CR, then the mementos, the books, cds, videos, and the other items having to do with your interests and hobbies, and then the things you will want for the kitchen, bedroom, etc.

Finding Your Home

Now you are back in Costa Rica, having visited a few months ago and been driven around the areas where you might want to live. If you were satisfied with your guide when you visited here, contact him or her again and tell them you want to first find a good *aparthotel* or small hotel in the area where you want to find a place to live. (I am assuming you will rent first since **you have to establish a corporation before you can purchase a home here**. Also, you must apply for permanent status under the *Rentista* category). My suggestion is to stay in an *aparthotel* as your base of operations.

A word about the U.S. government and associations here. Initially, we had thought to go the U.S. Consulate in San Jose to get lots of helpful information about the country. But we got busy finding a home and did not get there for three months. (Don't think you can go to the Embassy – that is apparently a policy place and not for American visitors) When we did go to the U.S. Consulate and ask for some information the young lady behind the glass partition first said they did not have any information, then started searching around and finally came up with a few printed pages of lawyers names and two pages of disclaimers about living in the country. Worthless information. As a contrast we were certainly treated most kindly by the Costa Rica Immigration people. They were very helpful in getting the forms we needed and in telling us what we had to do after we had experienced difficulty with our first immigration attorney and decided to proceed with the process ourselves for a time.

There are many business and social organizations and associations in CR. Joining a few of them will certainly give you more information about living here from those who have the experience. ARCR has a monthly weekend seminar featuring experienced speakers who will give you much insight on the requirements of moving here. You can join book clubs, bridge clubs, little theaters, business associations, just plain social clubs, golf clubs, and many more. We did not go to Chamber of Commerce, feeling we had no need for a business-oriented organization.

Back to finding your home: Purchase the *Tico Times*. This paper has advertisements for sales and rentals of homes and apartments of all kinds, sizes and costs in a great many areas of Costa Rica. It will give you some idea of how the house rental business works when you can call the ads and discuss the houses over the phone with an English-speaking person. You can make appointments to see those places that sound good to you. But remember, there are dozens more apartments and houses for rent in the local CR newspapers – *La Nacion*, *La Dias*, and the *La Republica* are good papers for ads.

Ask your guide to look for house or apartment advertisements in those CR Spanish language newspapers and to explain them to you when he finds one in the area of interest. Our guide sat with us for about two hours each morning calling ads on the telephone, getting information about the places, and then directions for the ones that sounded interesting to us. When you get into the rural countryside it becomes an interesting challenge to figure out just where the place may be. Just **make sure your guide has a cell phone** as he or she will surely need to call a few times as you try to find exactly where the place is! Our guide admittedly had a problem telling east from west and it became hilarious after the third phone call and hearing her say "Is there a group of palm trees on the corner near a tree stump?"

Take the time to look at many houses before you decide on one. Just make sure it meets all your requirements as to the house itself, where it is situated, the view, the other houses nearby, the town it is in or nearby, etc., etc. You never have to say any more than "Thank you very much" after you have seen a place, then leave to talk it over. The chances are it will not be rented in the days you need to see a dozen or so places in the area in which you have selected to live. Of course, there is always the possibility that you will find "your" place the first day or two, and the search will be over.

It is important to know that in Costa Rica the house rental leases are written for three (3) years to be legal. So the place you get should be one you really want to live in for a few years at least. However, leases in CR are generally written in favor of the lessee, so if you move into a place you find unsuitable after one year, you will most probably be able to break the lease without penalty. If you leave within one year it will probably cost you your deposit of one month's rent, or whatever security deposit you gave. This is why many people choose first to live in an apartment with a month, three or six month's lease – so they can take all the time they want and find just the perfect permanent place. If you plan to do this, remember that you can only stay in Costa Rica for three (3) months and then you have to leave the country for 48 hours (take a trip to Panama or Nicaragua) then come back in and you are good for another three months. Also, there are many *aparthotels* with monthly leases at attractive rates. It may cost a little more to live for the first few months if you choose to do that, but it will give you all the time you need to find the right home.

As in any community anywhere, there are the grapevines among friends and neighbors about places that are on or are coming on the market for rent; there are postings at the *pulperias* (neighborhood markets); at the internet cafes and other stores where one can find listings of rentals and sales, and there are many, many real estate companies, large and small. This is important because a realtor will have many, many listings. Also, there are listings that do not advertise anywhere, but rely on local word of mouth. Such available homes are known in the neighborhood, so be sure and have your guide or realtor ask around. They may not want to, but we have found that many very lovely and furnished homes are available, but are not advertised.

In CR one does not need a license to be a realtor. All kinds of people are in the real estate sales business either full or part time – lawyers, retired Americans, Tico housewives (all working out of their homes or offices), and of course, there is the established realtor who has been doing it for many years, and who certainly knows the area in which he or she lives. We contacted a realtor the second day we started our search, asking our guide to find us one in the area in which we were interested. It turned out that she really did have a lot of places for us to see within our price range, some quite grand for the price, and some were little places in villages, overpriced and sandwiched in between stores. The chances are the realtor will not speak English, so you will need your guide to translate. And you will need him or her to ask all the questions that may pertain to the local area such as : "How often does the electricity go out? Does the telephone number come with the house? Is the house up for sale? Is there hot water in all bathrooms? Is the water pressure satisfactory? Can we get cable TV here? Is there internet access?" and many more. Too often a realtor will not answer the right questions, or will down-play a negative answer to get you to lease the place. (Sound like home?)

Once you find your house for the next year or years, you must usually sign a lease and pay the first month's rent and/or a security deposit. You should also insist that you pay your rent in American dollars (USD), **not colones**, the CR currency, because government regulation states that if you pay in dollars your rent cannot be increased over the life of the lease. Also, when you find a place that seems perfect for you and you think you will want to stay for many years, you should have your attorney include a clause in your lease that allows you to renew at the same dollar rental (and hope the owner accepts it). Obviously, there may be some negotiation about this because the owner may want some protection against the annual 10% inflation. Understand, it may take time for the owner to draw up a lease for you, for you to have it translated and then add your own requirements, then for the owner to consider them and to write up a new lease, etc., etc. We moved in after having a verbal agreement and a handshake and didn't get the lease signed for five months! The translation took time, the re-write with additions took time, and the owner took much time getting a lease together in the first place. Nothing moves fast here. It is, however, recommended that you sit tight until you get the lease you want, have it signed, and the money transferred before you move in!

When the landlord presents you with a lease, be absolutely sure you give it to your CR attorney to review. And have it translated into English for you! He may defer as not necessary ("I can read it to you") because he doesn't want to take the time. There may be conditions to your particular lease – such as the owner has the right to sell and give you only 30 days notice, which is hardly desirable. Your attorney will discuss what changes you should have and should discuss them with your landlord. We just happened to find a very honest Tico/American couple who have acted with utmost integrity from the moment we first talked to them. To counterbalance that, we have heard of many cases of problems when couples moved in before signing the lease, OR, where they signed a lease in Spanish and found out later it said things they didn't like! So be advised.

From your first day in CR, when you change some dollars into *colones*, you will find you will need to quickly learn the values of this currency. *Colones* coins come in 5, 10, 20, 25, 50, 100 and 500 denominations. At the end of each day, even with a little shopping, your pockets will be heavy with metal! The paper denominations are 1000, 2000, 5000, and 10,000 *colones*. However, it will be prudent for you to open a savings account in one of the banks – either a government bank such as the *Banco Nationale*, or one of the private banks such as Interfine Bank or ScotiaBank – which now owns Interfine, so by the time you read this all the banks may be "Scotia." **In CR you cannot open a checking account unless you are a resident**. We have found, however, we really do not need a checking account since we can use the bank debit card at all the 24 hour ATM's, and they are everywhere. Remember that you must save all receipts of all transactions because you are responsible for spending a minimum of $600 a month in *colones*, although no government clerk has ever asked us for an accounting when we renewed our *cedula* – the permanent residency card.

That you may stand in line for thirty minutes at one of the larger government banks waiting to simply make a deposit or a withdrawal is true. This is partly because everyone pays the electric bill, the telephone bill, the water bill, and the cable tv bill at the bank! All the bookkeeping on your account is done at the teller's window when you present him with a request. This does take time.

And there will be twenty or so Ticos who are doing the same thing. When we were new in CR we would stand in a bank line for 45 minutes to get a traveler's check cashed and to inquire about our electric and telephone charges. As an aside, we have found that **traveler's checks are not popular**. Most banks will not cash one larger than $300.00, and you will find some resistance to cashing even the $20.00 check at stores because it will take around a month for the recipient to get his cash. **Travel with enough colones in your pocket to pay for a few days expenses**. Keep in mind as you read this that living here means a much slower pace, and "time" has not the urgency it has in the U.S. We do not mind the waiting. We have nothing to rush to. Admittedly, many expatriates use a private bank because there are fewer lines – most Ticos use the government banks.

Be advised that unless you are seeking a home near the ocean you will find few homes with air conditioning, and those will be pricey. At the ocean as elsewhere, most homes or buildings of any kind will **not** have air conditioning. Since the climate is so mild throughout CR, from 70 to the 80's degrees (except at the beach), no heat or air conditioning is required. In many areas you will find a home as simply a wood structure – wood floors, walls, and ceilings – with interior walls about 10 feet high, and an interior ceiling of 15 to 20 feet of a roof of corrugated red metal sheeting. The conventional construction of room ceilings in each room are the most prevalent, however. The smaller and inexpensive typical Tico homes are built of concrete blocks with the metal roof. The grander homes can have any amenity you require – large rooms, grand entrances, balconies, etc. In any case, when you are looking at a house, look to see if it has a crawl space above the ceiling, and ask if there is any insulation (there won't be in most cases) because when it rains hard, the din on a tin roof will mean you won't be able to talk above a shout until the rain stops.

The question asked by most Americans is "Can the country sustain a continuing inflation of 10% per year?" In my opinion, after talking with Ticos and North American residents here, and reading about the financial health of this country in the *Tico Times*, the answer is "Yes." This country is growing so fast that it will settle down in a few years time and so will inflation. If you are concerned, keep the bulk of your assets in the bank in dollars, or keep it in your American bank (I recommended you do keep money in your U.S. bank), or in Panama or Belize (as some Americans do) or the Cayman Islands if you want to go the "off-shore" route. It does seem that the U.S., and the World Bank (it recently lent the major *Banco De Costa Rica* $900 million), will provide CR financial support if it becomes necessary. And now with CAFTA (Central American Free Trade Agreement) having passed, it will be more prone to provide financial assistance should it become necessary. That CR has a large debt to the World Bank (financed largely by the U.S.) is also true. But be sure that the debt does not loom large in the American government's eyes, with its three trillion dollar budget. Plus, the U.S. will always need to have this country as a stable example of an open democracy in Central America. The phrase here is: "When America sneezes, Costa Rica catches a cold," to emphasize the dependency CR has on the U.S. Indeed, 80% of the gross national product is shipped to the U.S. or is from tourist dollars coming from the U.S. Tourism is now the major income producer for this country. There is a dependency to be sure.

However, CAFTA will open up Costa Rican business to American competition, for better or worse for the Costa Rican farmers and institutions, but that means a greater economic stability through much heavier American investment. I personally have little concern about the financial health of this country. In the past year Caribbean countries exported over $16 billion in goods to CR, and CR wound up with a $53 million trade surplus. There will be growth problems, to be sure, but there is an innate stability in the agricultural, health care, education, communication, and transportation systems that cannot be denied. That Americans are investing many millions of dollars in this developing nation is obvious from the beach communities to the Central Valley cities to the mountain resorts. American financial investors see financial opportunity here, not the reverse.

To those who are seeking an apartment, either to rent while you find your bearings, or if you plan to rent permanently, there are dozens of options. Apartments are available from spacious luxury accommodations in San Jose and the several small cities and towns nearby, and at several beach areas, from $1500 a month or more, with condominiums in the same category. And there are small, one bedroom apartments costing $300 and $400 per month in all areas. Apartment seekers should carefully decide first the location you want,. then the type and size apartment you need, then see several in that area. You will be able to find exactly what meets your desires, I am certain. It is still a buyers market in rentals of all kinds and prices, and the forecast, with all the construction planned and started, is that it will be so for years to come.

Apartment amenities such as Jacuzzi, balcony, first floor yard and garden, ultra modern kitchen, elevators, even air conditioning (at the beaches) are not uncommon, but you will pay for them. The trick is to find a desirable place that fits your dreams at a rate that fits your pocketbook. It can be done. Just keep looking until that place surfaces. An established realtor will be invaluable in this circumstance. Be assured, everyone will know someone who has an apartment available! When we got on the bus at the airport to go to the hotel the night we arrived, the driver asked "You look for place? Me uncle with fine apartments, here's card. Telephone tomorrow I take you." Even the tour guide working at the booth in the hotel will mention that he knows of some fine apartments or houses available at "very low cost."

A note on the terminology used in the ads. You will see *fincas* (farms) advertised in the *Tico Times* and your realtor will ask you if you are interested in a farm. The word "farm" in CR, when the location is in or near a small community, can mean a house with a large surrounding lawn of up to an acre in size. It does not mean a farm with cows and chickens and a hay field. It simply means more land than is usual around the house, or that it was a farm and was broken up into large lots with houses built on them. You will also see that properties are advertised in meters. Nowhere will you find how many square meters the interior of the house is (much less that figure in square feet). The size advertised is the size of the whole property of land on which the house sits. You can get an indication of the house size by the fact that it has 2 bdrm, 2 bth, or a 1 bdrm/bath. But you will always have to visit the place to see the house – and how large are the rooms! Apartments are always advertised by the number of bedrooms and baths, and sometimes mentioning the lvgrm, dnrm (not often), office. Family rooms seem to be non-existent, so don't look for that much space.

There are real agricultural farms – *fincas* – to be had, to be sure. You will see coffee farms, pineapple farms, and banana farms, fern farms, teak farms, and sugar cane farms advertised. They are usually of very large acreage, and the cost is in the hundreds of thousands of dollars. A word of advice: if you plan to come and invest in a going business property such as a pineapple or banana or coffee farm, **be wary**! We know of more than a few Americans who have lost many thousands through investing in a great-sounding growth potential business only to have the venture go broke within a few years. Mismanagement, corruption, and just plain stealing were the cause. In addition, you are at the mercy of the world markets for these agricultural products. Great profits last year do not mean good profits this year. Incidentally, talapia fish farms are growing in popularity here, thanks partially to the growing U.S. interest in farm-raised salmon and shrimp.

When looking for a house, whether city or country, farm, condominium or apartment, you should also know that the rooms – all the rooms – in Tico houses are small by U.S. standards. Ticos are smaller people in size, the men averaging 5'4" to 5'7", the women averaging several inches less. Bedrooms are considered spaces only to sleep in, so there is room for at most a queen size bed with the "dresser" built into the wall, or a free standing armoire, and maybe a straight chair, and no other space. Living rooms are also typically small, even 10' X 12' in the smaller two bedroom houses. And, of course, the kitchens are usually quite narrow with a 9 cu. ft. "fridge" and an electric stove. There are not many gas stoves used in the newer construction. We only saw one home with gas, and that house was way out of our budget. In rural areas you may be able to get a gas stove with bottled gas available, if you insist on it. We found early on – in our home with an electric stove – that we needed a small two-burner portable gas stove for those MANY times when the electricity goes out.

Now for the main consideration, and the one that gave us much consternation when we started looking at houses to rent. In an earlier chapter I mentioned what comes with an unfurnished house – nothing! And in the "partially" and "fully" furnished places you will have to buy more bed clothing, towels, kitchen appliances, dishes, silverware, etc., etc., etc. And, as Toni said in more than one place, "The overstuffed sofa and chair looks like vintage 1890." A bit dramatic, but indicative of the fact that the furniture is not going to be what you are used to! And you will have to supply everything needed for a reasonably accommodating household. When you are considering what to take with you in moving to CR, and plan to rent a house, you will need everything to "make a house a home" except what is described in this book. For you apartment seekers, you have a better chance with the newer "furnished" apartments to get a washer and dryer; otherwise there will not be much difference. BUT, you have to ask about **everything**. This culture does not offer suggestions (that would be rude) or tell you what you need to know (that would be impolite), so you have to ask every question you can think of.

So there you have it. Now you know how to go about finding the area in which you want to live, how to find a tour guide, get a realtor, and what to look for in finding your ideal place.

A word about the homes you will see. All of them, and I repeat **all**, have either iron bars on the windows, plus an eight to ten foot high iron fence around the property with a large iron gate at the entrance. From the smallest domicile to the grandest estate, you will see ironwork protecting the home. It is so common and one really becomes so accustomed to this situation that the ironwork becomes part of the architecture. Each property, large or small, has it's own distinctive design worked into the fence, and each fence is usually painted the color of the home, which will be in lovely shades of blue, many shades of green, some yellows and pink, even some purple, and tan, and white. Even the meanest home will have this iron protection. You will also see that the grander homes may add razor wire to the top of the fence as added protection.

Cities, Towns, and Villages

I have gone into the places you might consider in Costa Rica in earlier chapters. I did not mention much about Cartago (east of San Jose), or about the middle of the country (small villages), or about the southern half of the country. The main living is to be found in the communities near San Jose, and in the hills surrounding the Central Valley. Of course, if you are beach prone, then go to the communities mentioned there.

By the way, you should learn difference between miles and kilometers, and yards and meters, because everything here is in km and mt. Also, you should study the map that indicates the seven provinces. Since there may be several communities with the same name, such as Santa Barbara, all communities are formally identified as "Barva De Heredia" indicating that Barva is in the Province of Heredia – same thing as you naming your state after the town in which you live. As stated in the intro, this book centers around San Jose in the Central Valley, and on the southwest and western *playa* (beach) areas. Americans seem to want to live either in the Central Valley (S.J. being the center) or at a beach area. The other cities, large and small, come in for visits – native and tourist – but only a small proportion of immigrants choose to live in the more remote and small rural communities, preferring access to the amenities that the more populated areas have. After living here for a year or so, however, you may find you want to move to a remote area and enjoy a more indigenous lifestyle. Just make sure it has the telephone, internet, and cable capability!

This culture of personal responsibility has given Costa Ricans an individual dignity that is most appealing. By and large, each home, from the grand estate to the most modest small cement block house, has a neat and clean appearance, painted in a colorful hue, always landscaped with neat lawn and trees, shrubs and flowers about. Driving through a small community one enjoys the ambiance of brightly colored houses, small next to large, stores here and there, and flowered shrubs everywhere. There is indeed a dignity to the Tico lifestyle.

More About People

A word about the senior citizens of 70 years and above, called *tercero edad* (third age) here. They are highly regarded in this country. When a senior acquires the permanent resident status, he or she is accorded many perks, from free bus rides throughout the country (you do have to go to the proper agency and wait in line for the free passes), to no standing in the long lines at the banks, to a whopping discount on the local airlines, special event discounts, and more – another signal that this country has concern for its people. Also, while it is true that most of those emigrating here from North America have been senior citizens, there are more and more younger people and families coming to live in Costa Rica.

One does notice every skin color possible in the indigenous population. There are few black people in the Central Valley area as they mostly live in and around Limon on the Caribbean side, their ancestors having arrived there from Jamaica and the other islands for work a century ago. They speak English, but also maintain their native language. There are some Chinese and other Asians, but few Middle Eastern people or people from India. I would say that the average skin color of the Tico is a lovely tan to brown shade, and one can recognize the descendents of the indiginous "Indians" of a few centuries ago with particularly high cheekbones and flat facial features and a darker skin tone. You will also see that there are around 500,000 Nicaraguans in CR who have a darker skin tone. With high unemployment and a $.50 per hour average wage in Nicaragua, *Nicos* come here to pick coffee beans. The concern for the immigrant population of Nicaraguans is certainly analogous to that of the U.S. for its Mexican immigrants. One can also find fair-haired, blue-eyed descendants of the Dutch, English and American settlers who came here a century ago.

There are, in small pockets here and there, very poor tin shack houses, as can be found in any city in any country. In every village and town there are men who work by the hour and day doing just about any task, and they are hardworking and competent. While it does prick the conscience of a more affluent North American, all are grateful for the 750 colones per hour (about $1.50) offered to a laborer, even the housekeeper. Unemployment is running about 7%, not an extraordinarily high percentage, and one the country is seeking to improve.

As in all Central and South American countries, *futbol* (soccer to us) is a dedicated passion. Every school, village, town, city and country has it's *futbol* team, and games are constantly being played in the stadiums in every location. Some venues are small with few bleachers, some are grand 20,000 seat concrete bastions that rock when major teams come to town to play. The local and cable tv is full of games being played around CR as well as those in Europe and South America. There is some interest in baseball and in tennis, but no football as we know it. Golf is a sport with growing interest. There are now several courses throughout the country, and more are planned. The country clubs in and around San Jose enjoy fine reputations, as well as some in more remote locations, Guanacaste on the Pacific among them. For fisherman there is virtually every kind of sport fishing one could wish for. Some of the finest deep sea fishing in the world is offered on the Pacific side off the southern part of CR where marlin, tuna, sailfish, and other large game fish are to be found. There are many modern and well-equipped boats available for the most discriminating sportsman. In the rivers and lakes one can find the usual lake fish of trout and bass and more. Many splendid lodges are available for the dedicated angler, and the travel books are replete with places to stay.

I reiterate a note about "time" because that seems to be a real frustration to *gringos* who come here and can't understand why a housekeeper will show up an hour late for work. To a Tico, "time" is unimportant. Sometimes I have thought the adopted philosophy of this country is the saying, "If there is no time, then every moment is forever." Admittedly, when a Tico tells you he will deliver something *manana* he sincerely means to do it when you think he means – tomorrow. But in the Spanish used in Costa Rica, *manana* literally translates to tomorrow morning, tomorrow, or after tomorrow. So when you get your delivery three days later, everyone is happy because (a) it was delivered, and (b) because it was reasonably within the agreed date. You will not find a Tico refusing to deliver something because he must be paid first, or because he does not want to do it, or for any other reason. Even if he does not plan to do something he may say "Yes," and you will be left standing. But usually if a Tico says he will deliver something to you it will be done. Maybe not on your time schedule, but you will get the delivery, for sure. In other words, we have found that the Tico word is good.

It also must be said that to your reliable, knowledgeable, and recommended attorney, time has not the relevancy you may be used to. If he says he will translate your lease immediately, it may be done that week, or the next. Or the next. It will be done, of course, and accurately, but not promptly, because nothing seems to have any urgency here. Nothing seemingly has a priority ranking here – from returning a telephone call to writing a legal document. If translating a lease (regardless of when it was promised) is less important to an attorney than dealing with a real estate transaction (so many of them sell real estate too), then the translation is pushed aside. It does get frustrating when everything else seems more important than what was promised, but when you get into the rhythm of the country, all will fall into place, and you will learn to expect a document, delivery of an item, or a telephone call when it comes, and not before.

The Government

This is a country where there are far fewer government regulations. One can, in most areas, build a chicken house in the back yard without a permit, add a room to your house without a dozen city bureaucrats showing up to see if you are complying with some code or other; where the cable tv installer climbs the nearest electric poll and hooks up his line and strings the wire to your house. It reflects on the general attitude that still is strong in the rural countryside that each person is responsible for his or her own actions. By and large this country puts the emphasis on the individual's responsibility for his or her own actions. You are responsible for what you do, not someone else. For me this is a wonderful credo for living. It makes each person more independent, which to me is freedom.

It seems to me that this culture, rooted in personal responsibility, has not previously had the basis of law that enacts legislation because of fear that "something might happen." The people here have not lived in fear. The government has not in the past much concerned itself with the "possibility" of problems. Admittedly this is changing as the "outside" world comes closer. Today, it is a culture that is gradually changing due to the economic pressures that come with growth and more international alliances. This democracy acts like any other, it seems – political wrangling and posturing over every bill introduced in the Legislature. Laws here are now being enacted to protect animals, to protect spouses from abuse, to require people to wear seatbelts, etc. If you want the government to instruct you how to live your life more safely, it is slowly but surely coming about as CR looks to the U.S. for their model. In many ways it is a shame because the "individuality" character of this country is being lost.

There is a strong opposition Libertarian Party in CR that usually opposes any proposal the current administration puts forth, whether such proposal is beneficial for the country or not. This causes delays in everything from construction contracts on roads to providing for school desks, and more. The government needs an increase in taxes to pay for the needed infrastructure improvements, but the Libertarians oppose any tax increase. I have yet to see any alternative proposal put forth by this opposition party that will assist in forwarding the infrastructure development and that will help resolve some of the problems the country faces because of the rapid growth and expansion. But, all in all, things do eventually get done here, and the country is adding technology and gradually providing improvement in many sections of the economy. Ten years from now this country will be far more advanced technologically, with very good infrastructure, but it will also be a much more expensive place to live. And, the problems that will come before everything gets modernized and in place will be legion!

It seems that about every other year a bill is introduced in the legislature to raise the *Pensionado* required income upwards from the current $600. The sponsoring legislators proclaim that they do not want "poor people" coming to CR. Keep in mind that the majority of immigrants come from Central and South American nations, not Canada, the U.S., or Europe. In my judgment it is possible that some type of increase in these two areas will be enacted in a year or two as the country grows economically. It is possible that an increase in the *Pensionado* Status from the required $600 a month will be legislated to perhaps $800 or even $1000 a month. Or, it may be that no action will be taken.

The recently signed CAFTA Agreement – Central American Free Trade Agreement – will do much to increase trade by CR throughout the Central Americas, and with the United States. That it will help the U.S. bring goods in by lowering tariff barriers is true. It will also allow for eventual competition by the U.S. in the now-CR-government-controlled communication and insurance areas. Whether this will mean increased costs, as many argue, or whether it will simply mean more competition and better service is up for debate. The tariff and duty changes CAFTA requires will be adapted slowly, with gradually increased coverage over the next ten years.

There is also the recent Caribbean Trade Pact – CARICOM – which Costa Rica signed with 14 members of the Caribbean community. Only the Bahamas are not represented in this pact. The CARICOM countries are the fourth largest importers of CR goods, and a trade pact with them where 95% of CR goods are admitted duty free is certainly beneficial to this country. It opens a market of 15 million people to this country of 4 million.

As in all bureaucracies, there are government departments, commissions, offices, and agencies *ad infinitum*. The business community must always be alert to the pronouncements of the "Foreign Trade Promotion Office", and the Ministry of Economy, Industry and Commerce, and the National Insurance Institute, among others.

In December all government activity comes to a halt. School children are on vacation and most of the activities of government, if not closed, slow to a snail's pace. The observation of Christmas begins the first of November with traditional decorations and music blaring in the stores from that point on

The other major Holiday is Easter Week. Some institutions and businesses close for the entire week leading up to Easter Sunday. However, virtually every government agency, banks and businesses all close on the prior Wednesday. There are Christian observances from Wednesday through Easter Sunday.

Travel & the Beaches

In the dry season – summer – the few major airlines that fly into Liberia (for beach destinations) have increased their regular scheduled flights. Liberia is the airline "gateway" (meaning it is closer) to the Pacific *playa* areas of Puntarenas, the Golfo de Nicoya, and the peninsula across the gulf with its plethora of marvelous beaches. Also, there are small airports throughout Costa Rica served by local commuter airlines.

While not much has been said in this book about the Caribbean side of the country, you should know that excellent beaches and resorts are to be found south east of Limon, the principal port city of Costa Rica, down near the Panama border, and around Puerto Viejo. One and a half hours southeast of Limon are the beaches of Cahuita and Punta Uva. There are also some lovely islands in this area with small but excellent resorts for the vacationer.

Many travelers come here for the extraordinary visits to the tropical rain forests. On canoe and boat trips, one can stay in very accommodating lodges to enjoy a beauty that is fast disappearing in the world. These exceptional areas are well-documented in the travel books, and I would urge you to consider a visit to these more remote and exotic locations to understand what Costa Rica has to offer. When one lives here it is remarkable to me that such exceptional beauty is available for the modest price of a bus ticket and a night's lodging.

As well as the wonders of the countryside, there are dozens of small delights – from special coffee houses in Escazu to lodges in the rain forests run by expatriates from many countries. These small and sometimes unheralded adventures offer many pleasurable and secluded opportunities for travelers and tourists. A listing of a few of these places can be found at the end of this Supplement under "Special Places." It would be worth your time to look at them and find them on the map for visiting as a tourist or a resident.

Climate

While I may have dealt with this in a cursory way in the preceding chapters, a discussion of the climate is worth reviewing because this is one of the main reasons so many people come here to live. There is, and travel books never talk about this, a "windy" season in December and January. You should also know that the sun rises a little after 5:00 AM and it is dark at 6:00 PM, Central Standard Time. Most Ticos here do rise shortly after 5:00 AM and they retire early. All year. I am reminded of Franklin's dictum about "early to bed and early to rise."

As I mentioned at the outset in this book, one of the first things you will hear is that there are ten different climates in CR. Indeed, San Jose is generally hotter than surrounding communities, with Santa Ana being warmer than Escazu, which is higher up on the mountain. Cartago is flat and warmer, Heredia is hilly and cooler. Any mountain area from 4000 to 7000 feet is much cooler at night. Limon, on the Caribbean Coast, is much warmer and the Pacific seaside communities are certainly warmer in the dry season and have but a light breeze at most times. North and west of San Jose in the Poas and Barva volcano mountains areas one will find cool winds, and earthquakes once or twice a month early in the year, and will certainly experience very heavy winds in December and January – wind gusts up to 60 and 70 mph, mostly at night. I should say, however, that the weather here is always an anomaly at any given time, just as it is anywhere else. In March last year we had heavy winds for days. Houses do shake, rattle and roll with wind and quake. There are ten volcanoes in CR, all of them but two are dormant, one exception being the heralded Arenal Volcano, which to the delight of the thousands of tourists who visit each year, many nights has a spectacular eruption. The Barva Volcano, on which we reside, shakes and rolls several times during January and February. The Poas Volcano is the most visited tourist sight in CR, but sometimes you can make a trip to look down into the steaming crater and get turned away because it is shrouded in mist – or is spewing acid gasses that are dangerous. I might add that recent scientific studies on Arenal have shown that it is becoming a "possibly dangerous place to live" in that a serious eruption could happen at any time! When you visit, they make you back your car in the parking space so you can have a quick getaway!

As mentioned, we live now at 6000 feet and it is invariably 70 degrees in the daytime and 60, even in the 50's at night. Many nights in the "transition" months (November and December) we have a fire in the fireplace, and we still sleep under blankets at night in the "summer" of March. The sun is certainly hot in the daytime, winter or summer, but it seems that our daily temperature is almost always 70. It is sometimes amusing to hear someone from another community tout his climate saying, "We have much cooler breezes in Escazu", (or Santa Ana, or Grecia, or any town in the mountains). Everyone's climate is always better, it seems. The local pride coming in. To sum up, it would seem appropriate to say that there is an even tropical climate, warm in the daytime and cooler, if not cool, at night, no matter where one is. And I would add that almost everywhere, except sometimes in the cities, one will feel a soft breeze.

Health Care

This topic has been covered in earlier chapters. Suffice it to say that CR health care is considered the best in Central and South America and possibly among the best in the world. As a senior I joined CAJA – the national health care system – and it cost me $18 a month. I had to wait for this insurance until I had obtained my Residency Permit (good for 2 years, and then perpetually renewable). Every city, town and village throughout Costa Rica is served by the CAJA. As with any government controlled national health care system one may have to wait a month, or more, for a visit to the hospital for a non-threatening surgery, or for a check-up, if one does not wish to go to a private physician and pay the nominal fee. But for anything major, be assured that they will take you on the spot. And this government service is great for small cuts that need a stitch or two, or a simple fracture, because a CAJA Clinic can be found everywhere.

The private Cima hospitals in Santa Ana, and the Clinica Biblica in San Jose, are two of the best private hospitals one can find anywhere. I end this chapter with a story about a neighbor who recently had occasion to use Cima. As I discussed in the previous chapter about the people of CR, the gentleness and dignity of the people is obvious in the medical fraternity. The doctors and physicians and nurses are exceptionally well-trained and rigorously regulated. Many are trained in the U.S. and Europe. Because of the excellence and low cost of plastic surgery, there is a saying here that Costa Rica has a "little Hollywood" within San Jose.

The major CR medical insurance for employees is the National Insurance Institute, INS, a bureaucratized state monopoly whose insurance policies are recognized by both national and private medical facilities. This is available to permanent residents of the country and is most affordable. Another very good health insurance coverage is the new (started in 2003) lesser known and little talked about HHC - Health Horizons Corporation, established by the U.S government only a few years ago to be available to the needs of all U.S. citizens in CR. It has an exceptionally low $200 annual premium and also the assurance that all the health related expenses it provides will be paid by the U.S. government! This new organization is in San Joaquin De Flores in the Province of Heredia. You should investigate this insurance along with the others mentioned here when you get your Residency Permit. You should also be aware that there are programs that will supplement your Medicare! When we left the U.S. we cancelled our Medicare, but I would advise you not to do so until you settle in here and have your Residency Permit. You may find it wiser to keep it as an additional medical support. There are also some facilities that will take some U.S. health plans such as Blue Cross/Blue Shield.

We were surprised to see that almost every community has its "gym," a health and exercise work-out facility that has all the modern machines one can find in the U.S. Toni's monthly fee of $11 covers membership and unlimited use of her local club facilities. I might also add that there is a large emphasis on herbal medicines as cures for all kinds of common ailments. One can buy herbs in almost any market. We use herbs a great deal because we have long believed one should cure the source of a health problem instead of taking pills to cover up the symptoms. There are many herbalists, homeopathic physicians, and acupuncturists, especially in the Escazu area, the city, as noted before, that has the greatest concentration of U.S. citizens. Historically Escazu was the center for the medical practitioners of old, the shamans, the medicine women. As an aside, the first year here I got the *grippe* (greepay) – it seems that everyone in CR gets the *grippe* every year or so. One of the local Tico women suggested Toni should buy the "Noni" root and prepare it for me. Noni is very expensive in the U.S., but we found the root at one of the village outdoor markets for a few dollars. Toni prepared the evil smelling stuff, I took it religiously twice a day for three days and I was cured of the symptoms. This *grippe* was exactly like the "grip" I used to get as a kid – heavy cold, aches and sometimes nausea.

Life expectancy here is now 79 years of age – one more year than the U.S. – and the general mortality rate is one-half that of the U.S. for a variety of reasons – fresh fruit and vegetables in the diet being a main one, but be assured that the exceptional health coverage and facilities are also a good reason.

To give you another example of the health care here, one of our North American neighbors who has lived here for twelve years recently had a heart attack. He had let his CAJA insurance lapse due to carelessness (just forgot to send in his payment), but an ambulance came to this rural hillside, and took him to the Hospital Mexico in Santa Ana for surgery on a heart valve. He spent 1½ days in the ICU, two days in a semi-private room, and had a ride home in the ambulance. He has recuperated splendidly. The total cost was $1,645. I have not met any American here that has not said that the health care is absolutely exceptional. He renewed his insurance ten days later at the same monthly cost, there not being a concern or rate increase because he had a heart attack!

Living in Your Home

The electricity can go out from time to time, especially if you live in a rural area. It can be off for two minutes, or all day; it can happen twice in a day or not for many weeks and months. Just part of living. So, have a stock of candles, and be sure to purchase a lantern or two from one of the larger hardware or department stores. Just as we had to do in Santa Fe.

If your home is an older one there may be many minute cracks and corner holes by windows, sills, wall corners, etc. where the ants and small spiders and little crawlies can come in. A simple application of quick-dry plaster, or a judicious use of silicone in the cracks will take care of the problem. We are always asked by our U.S. friends if we have a problem with large spiders, lizards, and such, thinking that since we live in "the tropics" this must be the case. Not so. The largest lizard we have seen here was smaller than the one we had outside our Santa Fe home, and the spiders have been tiny. There are large and poisonous frogs in these hills – a hazard for the dogs who like to play with them – but we have only seen them when walking down in the forest by the river. And, there are tarantulas and scorpions around, but we have not seen any. As for snakes, we had a poisonous coral snake living in a stump next to the herb garden, but we didn't bother him and he didn't bother us. There is a strange tree-climbing animal that seems to be a cross between a groundhog and a squirrel (!) living in the trees behind the house. Also, there are innumerable different birds. Colorful to look at and with beautiful birdcalls. There are also birds nearby who live in holes in the ground.

If you live in the north, flat plains part of the country, it can get fairly dusty, so chances are you will really need some help keeping things clean. You can also get a fine dust film on things in the mountains north of San Jose when the wind blows. The shore areas have their own sand cleaning requirements, and domestic help can really be welcome.

Having promoted living in a more rural community, I have acknowledged that we do shop a lot at *AutoMercado*, a supermarket that carries almost everything American in food one could want. And, the ubiquitous Radio Shack can be found in most cities. It should also be mentioned that there seem to be an exceptional number of shoes stores and clothing stores. I counted seven shoe stores in one block in Heredia. Many stores of all kinds have well-dressed young people standing in front of them politely calling you to enter. Also, for clothing, in additional the numerous stores selling quality clothes, one should stop at one of the many "used" clothing stands that abound. A t-shirt one cannot tell from new is $.25, and other clothing is at the same level. My "almost new" Wranglers cost 500 colones ($1.25).

Other things are different here. Perhaps it is because CR is only 10 degrees from the Equator that the water spins counter-clockwise down the drain. We have found screws that were screwed in "backwards," and that a straw won't stay in your Coke bottle but slowly rises to the top, and that it is difficult to swim to the bottom of the pool – your body keeps wanting to surface. I have also found that if I spin rapidly clockwise, I get dizzy, but when I spin counter-clockwise, I do not. An interesting anomaly.

I should also mention the ubiquitous "sugar ants," the almost microscopic little ants that appear within half an hour after you have left a crumb or two on the kitchen counter. Keeping your counters and floors always clean will solve this little problem. It is said that every single home in Costa Rica has these little sugar ants.

They will get inside a jar of peanut butter – with the lid screwed down tight!

You will find it difficult to buy window curtains – which certainly will rarely be part of the furnishings that come with your home or apartment. After some searching in all the towns and cities near us, Toni finally bought the material and made her own. Later on we did find one store in San Jose that carried them. Previously I mentioned about finding a needle and thread at the local *pulperia*. But, with a little asking around, you will surely be able to find a seamstress who will do an excellent job for you.

Showers are the norm in most Costa Rican homes, not bathtubs. The showers are usually just adequate in size, and have a six inch tile rise as an edge. (If they made the rise twelve inches one could take a bath). Also, many houses do not have hot water at the bathroom sink. Why the hot water line is not run to the sink I cannot say, except that as one person told me, "If you have hot water for the shower, why do you need it for the sink?" Again, the inexplicable logic. You should check the house you are considering for the size of the water heater (too often too small), and if you are considering living in a more rural area, make sure there is a reserve water storage of adequate size with automatic pump to supplement the water flow if and when the water pressure drops in the dry season.

I will say that almost all of the houses we saw, when we were looking for a place, had plenty of closet and storage space. Some houses had armoires or dressers, and some had the clothes storing and hanging closets built into the walls. The latter is a nice arrangement and saves space.

Landscaping: If you are a lover of plants and flowers (as is Toni), this is the place for you. After a few years here we had eighty or so plants in the house and on the portico. Neighbors brought us plants, even trees, and suggested we take clippings and "stick them in the ground." Really. The saying is "Anything will grow here. Plant just before the rainy season and stand back." Of course, when planting in the dry season, as we have done from time to time, one must water everything every day.

Thus far we have planted hydrangea, camellia, gardenia, cactus, rubber plant, three different kinds of palm trees, banana trees (that do produce edible bananas once a year, then you cut them down and they grow again – fifteen feet high – in a year and produce more fruit). Also, china, pina (pineapple) mora, (like a blackberry), frangipani, fichus, mandarin orange (wonderful sweet oranges), lemon grass, aloe vera, riena del noche, bamboo, and about twenty more, the names of which I have forgotten or don't know.

Going Into Your Own Business?

I did! And the problems are legion! Although it might seem to the reader that I have given a lot of detail in the following recitation of my travails in starting a little business manufacturing children's wood toy blocks, be assured I really have left out many small and time consuming details involved in going into business in this country. I was told by a local businessman friend, "It will take three, maybe more years, to get a business established here. I wish you much success."

It all came about because I saw scraps of wood on the floor of my friend and former landlord who has a woodworking shop. I thought they would make great play building blocks for children in the PANI – the shelters for the homeless and abused children.

Toni had been going every Saturday morning to a shelter and spent the hours working with the children in all sorts of ways to give them a pleasant change.

I cut and sanded the blocks to several sizes, packaged fifty in a plastic bag and took them to the youngsters one day. They loved them! And whenever people would visit our house they saw them and bought a sack or two for their housekeeper's and gardener's kids as presents. So I thought "Maybe the toy stores in this country would like them too!" I did some local market research and realized that only one store out of the eight I had visited carried blocks, and they were plastic ones from China (where else). So I visited the major department stores – any big store that had toys, and got the name of the buyers in the central offices, asked a bi-lingual Tico to go with me, and visited those offices and showed my wares!

I started with the buyer for Hypermas – the largest food/ department store that was to me just like Wal-Mart in the U.S. I have mentioned earlier in this book that Wal-Mart did indeed soon buy the chain. The buyer spoke good English, however, and we got along splendidly. He was most helpful and suggested I must provide better packaging, and to come back in a few weeks with something colorful and compact that could be stored on shelves. I went to a fabric store in Heredia, purchased sturdy cloth and plastic and zippers, and designed bags for 50 and 25 blocks. Toni had noticed the local tailor in the village near our home, and to make a long, long story short, after much experimenting (he spoke not one word of English, and my Spanish was mainly nouns and sign language, but we found common ground), he produced bags that were functional and a visual attraction. The buyer liked them and, after settling on a price that would give me some profit and still meet the LOW prices that they required, said "I will take all you can supply."

Wow! A guaranteed volume even before I'm in business! Assessing the needs of a small woodworking shop, I borrowed the many thousands of dollars necessary from a friend, rented a small space for my factory, bought the woodworking equipment, hired two employees (with the assistance of my woodworking shop friend), designed the layout and storage racks for lumber, etc., negotiated the purchase of seasoned wood, and started in business.

Everyone, without exception, thought it extraordinary that an old *Gringo* would start a manufacturing company in Costa Rica! A good friend of ours said, "You have courage starting this when you don't know the business customs!" He proved to be right. I also visited a few small toy-store chains and immediately got an order from a buyer for six stores. A small order of fifty bags, to be sure, but a start, with the promise that there would be large orders coming for the Holiday season. Stores here do sixty percent (60%!) of their yearly volume in December! I should also mention that when I delivered the fifty bags of blocks I started to add the 13% sales tax to the invoice and the buyer quickly said, "Oh, you don't add that. It is not necessary for this first order." I was a bit puzzled, but he was the buyer and he should know the requirements, so I was paid without the tax. I was later told that the buyer would now add the tax to his sales, and thus making another 13%, and that should I make a profit this first year I would have to pay the government the 13%. I had been duped. But he was so nice and friendly and smiled at lot!

I hired a "toy designer" – a retired Dutchman and excellent craftsman – to make the prototypes for a hobby horse, a two-wheeled scooter, and chicken and duck pull toys. Working every day with my new employees, we soon produced splendid prototypes of my now expanded toy line. I hired my bi-lingual friend to take them around to the buyers and get some orders. I went back to Wal-Mart and showed them the new toy prototypes, and he promptly verbally gave me a fairly large order for the blocks only, to be completed in a month as I was not in full production of the new toys.

Then I had to find a box manufacturer to make cartons to hold six bags of each size as required by Wal-Mart, then take the bags and boxes to the HUGE warehouse and meet with the person who registers the boxes and gives the permits that allow one to sell to them. You have no idea of the minutia, the detail, the multiple regulations stipulating the exact requirements for anything and everything involved with selling to them!

Now I must give a summary on what it means to have employees. Workers in this people-oriented country take a job for one reason: to make enough to feed the family. Initially I had grandiose ideas about giving some stock to each employee – makes for a more dedicated worker, right? Well, that's wrong. The average worker does not understand nor care about company shares (which would mean potential share in profits). Nor do promises of a bonus mean anything – it is not in hand, so has no meaning. What a man receives at the end of the week is what is important! And should a bonus be given at the end of a good month, the employee will simply wonder why you are giving him the extra money. He will take it, and think you are a little tetched. And be assured that should a crisis require working on a Saturday or a holiday, even with paying double wages, the employee will not want to work. He may do it simply so he won't be fired, but will resent it, and resent you! Also, in every single instance, down to the smallest detail, you must give exact directions as to the work to be done and what day and week production must be accomplished . If you do not, your most reliable foreman will simply do the work the way he wants to – not unlike a housekeeper using a broom instead of a vacuum cleaner – which many times will mean doing the whole job over again. Also, when I started the business I was told that the workers must have a happy shop to work in, or else they will quit! Finally, workers expect the boss to be there giving directions at each step of the way. The most reliable foreman MUST have direct supervision! When the *patron* or *jefe* (boss) is not around the work slows down, the workers begin working on things they like doing, and production goes out the window.

And should a minor accident occur, such as a cut finger, forget putting a Band-Aid on the cut, the worker will want to be taken to the local clinic (you will have purchased the INS insurance for employees) for shots, stitches, bandaging, and maybe a sling, and be given the rest of the day off. With pay, of course. Remember that an employee costs run about 40% more than the salary or weekly hours, with all the add-on costs and holidays..

Back to the toy business. Visiting the major box manufacturers in this country I found they had a minimum order of 2000 boxes of each size! So I found a small manufacturer in a nearby city (another week lost) who works out of his home and makes boxes to spec. Higher charge, but with a little increase in the wholesale price I could absorb this added cost. Of course, the first order of 100 boxes were made a slightly wrong size and had to be done over – my cost! – even though the box man had done the measurements and the boxes now measured slightly less on one side. There is no such thing as returns due to faulty manufacture in this country!

So I was ready to go, and met once again – probably visit number ten – with my Wal-Mart buyer who promptly announced "I want a corporation to deal with, not just Alfred Stites!" So now I find a lawyer to have a corporation formed. Not difficult, but a detailed procedure that took weeks to have accomplished. A month went by as I took forms to this government agency and then that one for their myriad papers, forms, stamps, and certifications. They stamped this and that, each department sending me to another department for a stamp and/or approval of some form or other. Then back to the Buyer with the corporate registration who then required another form the lawyer did not tell me about, so I did the rounds of the government agencies again, finally getting everything correct for my friend the buyer. It only took another month.

Now, sitting in his office with much anticipation, he informed me that instead of the large order he had promised, he wanted a small order to "test the sales potential." I filled that order promptly, having had my little shop cranking out blocks by the thousand – I had hired two more employees to make sure I could fill the anticipated demand. I proudly showed my hobby horse, scooter, and pull toys, now in full production, to the buyer. He complimented me on the quality of the product, then said "I have ordered these toys in plastic from China, so I do not require them now, but I may want them later." I think he liked my ideas of a hobby horse and pull toys, so ordered them "on the cheap."

Then I went back to the buyer of the toy store chain who had asked me to return in two months for a re-order if the sales had gone well. After the many pleasantries one goes through here when seeing someone after a month or a day has passed, we got down to business. He smiled and said "Alfred, your blocks sold so well we are adding blocks to our line for all our stores. However, I have found a cheaper wood block made in Brazil, and I have ordered them. So I will not need your blocks. Thank you for coming to see me." I did not try and explain that the bags sold because of the very attractive packaging, and that how the product was marketed was the key, not the price! No point. At least he gave me a firm answer.

I will not detail here the many phone calls made, the many trips made to several toys store chains to interest them in my product. In every case, in every single case, I was told "I really like these blocks! And your hobby horse and pull toys are very attractive. I will want them, to be sure, but not just now. I think I may consider them for the Christmas season. Call me for an appointment next month."

As mentioned above, I had hired my bi-lingual Tico friend to visit all the toy stores in San Jose, and get me some sales. He was a mature, well-spoken, intelligent, handsome man from an old CR family, and if anyone could get sales, I was sure he could! I went with him to the first few stores to see how he presented the product, and was impressed with his sales ability. But every week he would report that the stores, every one, were really interested in the product, but they were not ready to buy now, but would do so in a month! I went through September, October, November, and into December with promises. I finally went to my WalMart buyer on a Thursday, ten days before Christmas. I asked for an order. He said, "How many bags of blocks do you have for immediate delivery"

"I have 385 bags of the 50 blocks, and 215 of the bags of 25" I replied, leaning forward in my chair.

"I will take 200 bags of 50 and 100 bags of the 25 size for delivery tomorrow!" He started punching numbers on the telephone, calling this and that department, warehouse, merchandise manager, inventory chief, and who knows who else, and when he had finished said "If you don't deliver these exact amounts tomorrow – Friday – it will be Saturday, and we don't take deliveries on the weekend, and then it will be Monday, and that will be longer than the 3 days we allow a vendor to deliver to us. If your delivery is not made tomorrow I will not be able to do business with you any more!"

Going to my shop I started setting aside the bags for delivery and found to my dismay that well over half the bags in my inventory had mold on the inside. I showed this phenomenon to my woodworking friend who said "You were sold green wood and mold grows in a closed bag in this climate!" My workers and I sat all afternoon checking every bag for mold and separating out those that could be delivered the next day. As I worked I rehearsed in my mind what I was going to say to my lumber supplier who had assured me he delivered seasoned lumber to me. It was too complicated to detail here, but the lumber mill delivered a cheaper and lighter wood than I ordered, and it was green. The lighter weight made me think it was seasoned. My fault for not watching every step of the process and questioning every detail. So, now I had to hustle around and find a delivery truck and driver, and the next day delivered the order.

Half my inventory at "one fell swoop!" This order, however, proved to be my swan song. After the mandatory paid-week vacation at Christmas, I started up again in January, and once again my Tico salesperson made the rounds of buyers in San Jose. Once again I heard the "I like your toys! But come back in a month." At the end of January I was running out of money, and being aware of the necessity to have enough to pay the salary severance, the severance vacation, the severance for … some other government requirements that are mandatory when one fires someone or closes a business, I paid my employees off and closed the shop. I remembered my friend's admonition those months before: "It takes years for a new business to take hold in this country."

This Christmas Season I will offer – at GREAT DISCOUNTS – the remaining stock of play blocks, hobby horses, and pull toys to any store and any person who wants them. I learned my lesson. I had a good time, I learned a lot, and I know now not to try and go into business in Costa Rica. I don't really understand how they operate. If I had the money for a three year operation, I probably could have eventually had a small, stable, growing toy business. Maybe. At the beginning of this book I remarked that these gentle people do not like to say "No." It is rude. So a buyer will not tell you that although the quality and price were acceptable, he was not interested in carrying a line of wood toys. He smiles and tells me what a fine product I have and that the prices will allow him a good profit, and to come back and see him again!

I say, "Ah, well, *c'est la vie.*"

Buying a House or Property

Your world just got complicated if you plan to buy property. As you may remember, I suggested you live here for a while to find just the right area/place/house. And when you do, buying the house requires:

1. A knowledgeable and honest realtor who will represent YOU and not the Tico seller!
2. A knowledgeable and honest attorney/notary skilled in, and very experienced in, real estate transactions!

To find a really good realtor I would consider those with a web site; those with a national, if not international reputation and clientele. A small town realtor may be the right one to find you a rental, but for buying I would suggest you need a larger scope.

Buying an existing house is fairly straightforward. You should, however, get an appraisal from a licensed person. Sellers here ALWAYS quote too high when *Norte Americanos* are asking. The *Colegio Federado de Ingenieros y Architectos* can supply you with the names of competent people. Your lawyer will check for liens, that the property is recorded in the name of the man selling it(!), that there are no other claims against the person's assets, and that the property is totally free for you to purchase. Your realtor should check that there is adequate and pure water, that there is a sewage or septic system, that there is adequate electricity in the area; he will look into what other construction is going up or liable to be built that may strain the existing infrastructure, that the roads leading to the property are not likely to cave in or be subject to landslides in the rainy season. You will have to find out about the telephone, the cable, and internet access.

One of the things you must recognize: sellers and realtors and lawyers are no different here than in the U.S. They will all want you to buy the property, so you must take NOTHING for granted. You must NOT accept a statement by the seller that you can easily get a telephone, or cable, or a heavier electric line, or that the house is **properly grounded** so that every lightning bolt doesn't close you down for a week. Have your realtor go to ICE (eesay), the electric company to verify the conditions. Most houses **are not** adequately grounded. You can save yourself a lot of expense later on by having an electrician ground the electric wiring correctly. Also, check that 220 voltage is where you will need it, such as if there is no dryer and if you plan to buy one you will need 220v. Or that the septic system works perfectly and does not need emptying, or that the water pressure is always high (find out where your water comes from!), or that there is hot water to the sinks in the bathroom. Check EVERYTHING! And be sure that if something needs being done or corrected have it done BEFORE you move in or you may wait a year of Tico time. And did I mention ROOF LEAKS? This is obviously an owner's problem, but you should have something in the lease about the roof being fine. Of course, both the lawyer and the realty agent may think you are the pickiest *Norte Americano* they have ever run across, but you just smile and insist. May I tell you about a seller pointing out the new dishwasher in the kitchen to prospective buyers and when they signed everything and moved in they found that it didn't work! Of course, if the purchase did not state in detail that all the appliances had to work perfectly, the new owner was soon scurrying around to find a competent repair man!

Things get very complicated here when one wants to buy property and then build on it. There is a standard procedure, of course, but you are really doing two transactions — buying land, and building a house, so there is double the red tape to go through. We know people who have come here with that in mind and then, after a few weeks of seeing what was required in this bureaucracy, they gave up and went back to the States. Buying the land means that a competent attorney will have to verify that the title is clear, that the zoning allows for housing, that the boundaries are correct, that any needed access is approved, etc. You must also have the soil tested for stability and drainage; you must check for water access, sewage necessities, and electric supply. When you build you must submit plans to the municipality for approval of the type of house you plan, for the architects and construction plans, you must have the necessary building permits, you must get approval for cutting any trees, and on and on.

As you can see, you will need to read a book written by a competent specialist before you make a decision to go ahead and build your own dream house on your own special piece of land! That is why there are so many planned communities – they will build your house reasonably in the design you want without your having to go through all that. And there are these communities going up all over Costa Rica – in the foothills, by the beaches, even in the more remote mountain areas.

Being a Newcomer

In trying to give you the details about moving here, I have not given much space to Toni's and my daily life, aside from what you can glean from my descriptions and comments. I can only say that as strangers arriving in a strange land, we were received very warmly. Three days after we moved into our house we were invited for Thanksgiving Dinner by an American/Tico couple. A week later we were told of a party that was to be given for us at a neighbor's house so we could meet all of the people who live around this hillside. We were invited by Tico neighbors to Christmas and New Years dinners. In spite of my trepidation we had a lovely time "conversing" with six Spanish-speaking couples, me using basic nouns and adjectives that sound similar in any Latin-based tongue, plus sign language, and Toni practicing her developing Spanish. We were also invited by the Tico owners of a resort just down around our hill to come any time and use the pool and tennis courts as their guests. In our first two months here we had evenings with several U.S. and Canada expatriates at small dinner parties and very large afternoon gatherings. Neighbors have invited us to use their car any time we like. We were received hospitably by both locals and expatriates alike.

As in any new place, however, when living in a new style/ type house, in a rural area, in a developing country, there have been minor challenges. It is not North America, and this country surely has its own character, and one must make adjustments. I trust you have enjoyed my recitation and are not deterred from making a trip here. Even moving here!

Useful Information

The following few places and things are just some of those we have found to be good. Some too high priced, but high quality; some rustic and low price, some just average quality but we liked the place or eatery.

Spanish Phrases You'll Need

First, buy a Spanish / English Dictionary! You'll need it all the time. Then look up and learn these phrases:

Please, good morning, good afternoon. Hello. How are you?. I am fine. Thank you. How much does this cost?, What is the charge? Where is …? What time is it? When will …… return?

Where can I find ...? No thank you, That is too much. Is this correct? seafood restaurant, good restaurant, more or less, I am sorry, I apologize, I will return, next week, my Spanish is not good, excuse me, clothes, house, furniture, food, water, shoes, umbrella, beach, hotel, for rent, buy, sell, bus, car, dog, cat, rain, sky, sun, ground, pencil/pen, paper, book, coffee, black, milk, dessert, number, name, bathroom, stove, shower.

Really not too many to learn to make life easier here.

A few hotels in and around San Jose
(If none of these strikes your fancy go to Costa Rica Innkeepers on the internet.)

Aurola Holiday Inn, (downtown) San Jose. Modern, complete facilities, good restaurant, casino. email- reservations@aurolahotels. com; 506/523-1260. single is around $100.

Hotel Best Western Irazu, western edge of San Jose. Modern, single is around $90. All modern conveniences, fair restaurant. 506/232-7910

White House, Costa Rica. Hotel, good restaurant, casino, spa. Upscale, but worth it. Oddly enough they also have Harley Davidson tours! Very good food, best views of the valley. Most everything is high end. (They pick you up in a new Hummer!) www.whitehousecostarica.com, 506/288-6362.

Hotel Monte Compana, north of Heredia. A "local" resort hotel, around $75 a couple, Tico-type restaurant, solid but good food, in the mountains with great views of the central valley. www. qualitycostarica.com.

Stan's Irish Pub, Zapote, on the east edge of San Jose. Not a hotel, but a new IRISH pub in this country. Great beers, and Stan Salas has made a friendly place to sample his 18 or so beers.

At the Beach

The Mansion Inn. A true-on Luxury place to stay in Manuel Antonio – the most popular visitor's site in CR! You can pay from $350 to $1,500 a night for splendid accommodations. And the food is supposed to be great (we can't afford it but maybe you can).

The Paradisus Playa Conchal Resort, playa Conchal. Upwards of $150 p/person, dbl occ. Nice new resort. Don't know the restaurant quality.

Manatus Hotel, Tortuguero (Caribbean side, north). Jungle, remote luxury and worth it, around $300 ea. dbl occ. total cost – all meals, guided excursions, etc. www.manatushotel.com, 506/239-4854

Hotel Luna Azul, at the upper edge of the Nicoya Peninsula. A New (since 2006) small, fine, special hotel with excellent food, right on the edge of a national forest. Lovely accommodations and reasonable – $100 / night..

Punta Marenco Lodge, Drake's Bay. Really remote for those who want a rustic lodge "on the edge." At the Pacific ocean near a village in the middle of Osa Peninsula. Near the world's most biodiverse

Corcovado National Park. A dbl is $150 / night including food; they have 4-day pkgs.; 15 cabins with mosquito netting; quality service, food, and accommodations. www.puntamarenco.com.

On your way to or leaving the Lodge, visit Paradise Tropical Garden near Rio Claro about 20 km north of Golfito – extraordinary fruits and trees you won't see elsewhere. http://paradise-garden. tripod.com.

Pelican Hotel, Esterillos Este, on the central Pacific coast south of Jaco. 12 rooms, swimming pool, air cond., nice accommodations, food, beach (but riptides), off-beat tourist spot.$55-70 (tax incl!) and the good food is reasonably priced. www.pelicanbeachfronthotel. com.

Rancho Naturalista Mountain Lodge. An exceptional Lodge in the middle of Costa Rica (about). On the Caribbean Slope 20 km SE of the village of Turrialba. More high end than most lodges in the forest areas, this provides what any serious birder wants. Plus horseback riding. $160 / person, dbl occ. incl. meals. www. costaricagateway.com.

Pure Jungle Spa, right down near the Panama border on the Caribbean Ocean, south of Puerto Viejo on Playa Cocles. This is a jungle spa with all manner of massages, treatments, facials, and on. Bungalows rent from $35 - $60 a night and accommodate from 3-6 people; the massages run from $60 - $100 depending on time. The beach is there with a lifeguard because of the rip tides. www.lacostapapito.com

Tamarindo, a few good places to eat when you go there: Breakfast Grinds – really good breakfasts and a bit pricy, but so is much in this town. Olga's Café, good eats, more reasonable prices, lighter food, on the Langosta Road. Gil's Place, another reasonable eatery with good food, also on the Langosta Road. For *bocas* (appetizers) try the Lazy Wave Lounge, just west of Hotel Pasatiempo. Pricy, yes, but good. And finally the Sunset Lounge Balcony and Bar, upstairs at the circle which is nice, and pricy. (When I say "pricy" I mean compared to regular Tico prices, not U.S.).

List of Restaurants
There are so many restaurants here, and so many good ones that you should buy the *Tico Times* book of CR's 300 restaurants. If you want to go to just one place and find six very good, a little pricy, but fine food restaurants, go to the Plaza Itskatzu (the old spelling of Escazu) just on the outside of that city and near the Cima Hospital. You will find several very different cultural offerings of quality.

The Tico Times Address
APDO 4632-1000, San Jose, Costa Rica. (506) 258 -1558. U.S. residents send mail to The Tico Times, SJO 717, P.O. Box 025331, Miami, FL 33102-5331.
The paper is printed in the U.S. also for prompt delivery.

The Association of Residents of Costa Rica (ARCR)
See: www.arer.net, email: arer@casacanada.net. Telephone: 506/233-8068 or 221-2053. They speak English and will be helpful. There is a fee to join – around $100, then there is a monthly fee of around $30 which includes a person's CAJA (government health

insurance). There are also private health insurances available which are much cheaper than in the U.S. As mentioned elsewhere, they have an excellent staff of lawyers.

What you will need to bring with you

Items needed for living in CR that are not easily obtainable:

Bedroom – high count bed linens, down comforters (for above 4000 feet), down pillows, bedspreads

Clothes – if you plan to spend much time in the lower areas bring a few pairs of shorts, jeans, t-shirts, and sandals, if in the hills and mountains bring sweats, heavier t-shirts, jeans, moccasins, socks and walking/hiking shoes. You will always need a nice pair of slacks, shoes, and a shirt.

Bathroom – special toiletries, elec. toothbrush, shoe trees, razors (even the cheap plastic ones are expensive here)

Living Room – any special furniture you care for – if it is a bit different you will not find it here; any knick-knacks that are special, pictures – both oils and watercolors without the frames – framing is very cheap here and the quality is not great but acceptable, for furniture go to the town of Sarchi to have it built to your specs. You'll see dozens of furniture stores around but too much will be Tico style which is overstuffed and often garish

Dining Room – Your own set of china, packed right – what is generally available is not high quality, and the good stuff is very costly. Bring your own silverware; you can buy the stainless flatware very reasonably; any other special decorative bowls and decorating accoutrements that are your taste and that you probably won't find here

Kitchen – the bugaboo of all expats. Bring as many small appliances as you can, stainless steel bowls from small to large, glass measuring cups, other measuring instruments, all quality carving knives, copper plated pots and pans

Garden Equipment (not easily found) – large hedge cutters, push lawn mower for small plots, electric trimmers.

For a list of Banks, Hospitals, Clubs, Churches, Synagogues, Associations, Golf Courses, and so many other institutions, resorts, areas to visit, hotels, places, operations, etc. just pick up one of the many travel books at any of the larger hotel shops. Many listings are also available daily in the *Tico Times* and other English speaking newspapers.

Did you like *Sidewalks in the Jungle?*

Do you need more copies for friends and relatives? Of course you do! Order directly from the publisher at www.geroproducts.com, through your local bookstore, or use the order form below (may be photocopied).

Also, you may be interested in our other books and gifts:

Qty __

Sidewalks in the Jungle: What it's REALLY Like to Retire and Live in Costa Rica by Alfred Stites - $35.95

This book deals with the reality of moving to, and living in htis beautiful and stable Central American democracy. Topics covered span from managing maids and gardeners to trips to the doctor and avoiding violent street crime.

Qty __

The Healthy Seniors Cookbook: Ideal Meals and Menus for People Over Sixty (Or Any Age) by Marilyn McFarlane - $19.95

Whether cooking for yourself, your spouse, or visiting grandchildren, this book features an easy-to-read, easy-to-use format that provides flavorful meals and simple, fast cooking methods.

Qty __

Seniors in Love: A Second Chance for Single, Divorced and Widowed Seniors by Robert Wolley - $19.95

This well-reviewed book deals with the emotional, financial, physical, and other relevant issues facing seniors when considering a new, intimate relationship.

The Greatest Companion: Reflections on Life, Love and Marriage After 60 by Robert Wolley - $19.95
Through prose and poetry, this book explores the joys of late-in-life love, provides reminders of what such a love needs to flourish, and reflects upon love's agelessness.

ABC's for Seniors: Successful Aging Wisdom from an Outrageous Gerontologist by Ruth Jacobs - $19.95
In this book, Dr. Jacobs presents the essentials that enable a reader to harvest life fully for creative, healthy, successful, vigorous, and meaningful aging.

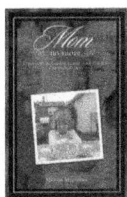

Mom No More: Coping With the Late-Life Loss of Adult Children - One Woman's Story by Mignon Matthews - $29.95
A widow is a woman whose husband has died and an orphan is a child whos parents are both dead, but what is a woman whose children are dead? There is no name for them, but they exist. The author lost both of her children after they were adults - her daughter Evie at 18 and her son Albert at 42. This is her story of coping with the depression, pain, anger, and injustice of outliving her beloved children.

Qty — *Seniors in Love* car magnet - $11.95
Show the world that love knows no age! An ideal wedding or anniversary gift! Measures six by four inches, in red, white, and gold. Removable. Fits any RV!

Qty — *"Grow old along with me"* mug - $9.95
Robert Browning said it, but it's as true today as it was 100 years ago! Illustration and quote, printed in black on both sides. Truly, *"the best is yet to be"*

Name   _____

Address   _____

City/State/Zip   _____

Please mark the products you want, and their quantity (Missouri residents only please add 5.25% sales tax).

There is no charge for shipping and handling, and all orders are shipped from Greentop, Missouri (population 427).

Send check or money order to:
Hatala Geroproducts
PO Box 42
Greentop, MO 63546

What makes Hatala Geroproducts different?

Hatala Geroproducts of Greentop, Missouri, was founded in 2002. An independent company, Hatala Geroproducts publishes books, games, magnetic signs, and greeting cards primarily for seniors. The focus is on relationships: with spouses, lovers, other seniors, grandchildren, and adult children.

• All products are "age positive", which means that they are respectful to seniors, and focus on the positive aspects of aging.

• All books are "larger print" for easier reading.

• Books are written by senior authors for senior readers.

• All products are developed with the help of academic gerontologists and seniors themselves.

• Hatala Geroproducts is dedicated to remain an earth-friendly, sustainable, carbon-neutral company.

We thank you for your continued support!

If you have any questions or comments, feel free to contact me personally at mark@geroproducts.com

Mark Hatala, Ph.D.
President, Hatala Geroproducts
Professor of Psychology, Truman State University

www.ingramcontent.com/pod-product-compliance
Lightning Source LLC
Chambersburg PA
CBHW030410100426
42812CB00028B/2896/J